MY AFRICAN HORSE PROBLEM

My Africar

ALSO BY WILLIAM F. S. MILES

Zion in the Desert:
    American Jews on Israel's Reform Kibbutzim (2007)
Political Islam in West Africa:
    State-Society Relations Transformed (ed.) (2007)
Bridging Mental Boundaries in a Postcolonial Microcosm:
    Identity and Development in Vanuatu (1999)
Imperial Burdens: Countercolonialism in Former French India (1995)
Hausaland Divided:
    Colonialism and Independence in Nigeria and Niger (1994)
Paradoxe au Paradis:
    de la politique à la Martinique (1992)
Elections in Nigeria: A Grassroots Perspective (1988)
Elections and Ethnicity in French Martinique:
    A Paradox in Paradise (1986)

Horse Problem

WILLIAM F. S. MILES *with Samuel Benjamin Miles*

UNIVERSITY OF MASSACHUSETTS PRESS Amherst

Printed in the United States of America

LC 2008034654

ISBN 978-1-55849-682-8 (paper); 681-1 (library cloth)

Designed by Richard Hendel

Set in Chaparral type by dix!

Printed and bound by Sheridan Books, Inc.

Library of Congress Cataloging-in-Publication Data

Miles, William F. S.

  My African horse problem / William F. S. Miles with Samuel Benjamin Miles.

    p. cm.

  Includes bibliographical references.

  ISBN 978-1-55849-682-8 (pbk. : alk. paper)—ISBN 978-1-55849-681-1
(library cloth : alk. paper)

  1. Nigeria—Description and travel.   2. Nigeria—Social life and customs.
3. Peace Corps (U.S.)—Nigeria.   4. Hausa (African people)—Social life and
customs.   5. Miles, William F. S.—Travel—Nigeria.   6. Miles, Samuel Benjamin,
1989– —Travel—Nigeria.   I. Miles, Samuel Benjamin, 1989–   II. Title.

  DT515.27.M55 2008

  916.6904'54092-dc22

  [B]   2008034654

British Library Cataloguing in Publication data are available.

Frontispiece: Sam on Sa'a, 2000.

To

Mother and Grandmother
"Meema" Helen Miles-Rayner,
Who Made Sure This Book
Happened

CONTENTS

FIGURES, MAPS, ILLUSTRATIONS

ACKNOWLEDGMENTS (and an explanation or two)

It was my mother who *noodged* me to write this book.

The problem was that I had recently begun another one, about a Reform Jewish kibbutz in the Negev Desert in Israel, and I felt duty bound to complete that project before throwing myself into this one. It had been a year since I'd taken my family to the summer inferno of the Jewish State, and the kibbutzniks were already impatient with me: *Where's the book already?* The tug between the two write-ups resulted in literary paralysis—not writer's block, but authorial indecision. National Public Radio (NPR) had already broadcast two of my commentaries about my African horse problem, and the story had already made the rounds among kith and kin and close Africanist colleagues. These included friends Larry Diamond and Jeffrey Liteman, both of whom accompanied me to one of "my" Niger-Nigeria frontier villages. During our '80's academic comic tragedy in northern Nigeria, Mallam Larry and Public Affairs Officer Jeff provided greatly appreciated R & R in Kano. So did Dr. Momodou N. Darboe. For believing that the readership would be much greater than just family and friends, I am pleased to acknowledge my editor at the University of Massachusetts Press, Bruce Wilcox, and my fellow Hausaphile colleague at U-Mass, Professor Ralph Faulkingham. Professor Paul Newman generously offered to check my "bush" Hausa against standard usage. For exercising *savlanut* (Hebrew: patience) for that other book, I thank the members of Kibbutz Yahel.

But back to my mother.

As with any normal, overprotective Jewish mother from New York, mine was absolutely horrified that, instead of going to medical or law school after college, I would join the Peace Corps and go off to live in the middle of Africa. (For that matter, I ought also to thank those half dozen élite law schools that, by rejecting me, rescued me from a post-Vassar life of jurisprudence.) When she could no longer resist my ultimate expression in youthful rebellion, Mother implored me to heed three warnings. Remember that my leaving for Muslim Black Africa, in 1977, coincided with seemingly frequent Palestinian hijacking of U.S. and Israeli airplanes as well as an upsurge in other anti-American and anti-Semitic terrorism.

"When you're over there," my mother intoned, "do not say you are an American."

"Yes, Mother."

"And do not," she continued, "reveal that you are Jewish."

"Yes, Mother."

"And lastly," my mother implored, "never tell them that you are *white!*"

It is to her everlasting credit that, twenty-two years later, Helen Miles-Rayner "allowed" me to take her ten-year-old first-born grandson back with me to Muslim Black Africa.

Were it not for his fifth grade teacher, Mr. William Foley of the Mildred Aitken Elementary School in Seekonk, Massachusetts, I'm not sure Samuel would have made it here as co-author. It was Mr. Foley who proposed that, in exchange for the days of school missed, Sam keep a diary of our trip together. Most of the italicized passages that appear below are entries from that diary; a few are elaborations that I asked him to add soon after we returned home.

All Things Considered, that stellar evening program of NPR, saw fit to broadcast my pre-departure reflections as Sam and I were on our way to Logan Airport on February 10, 1999. As a result, several other former Peace Corps Volunteers and friends of Niger contacted me with kind words of encouragement and nostalgia. To them, as well as to NPR and its local Providence affiliate WRNI, I therefore say: *Madalla.*

Over the years I have been able to share my African thoughts, horse-related and not, with esteemed fellow Africanists whom I have had the good fortune to befriend. They include Tony Asiwaju, Larry Bowman, Deborah Bräutigam, Ed Bustin, Barbara Callaway, Bob Charlick, Naomi Chazan, Peter Chilson, Andy Cook, Momodou Darboe, Larry Diamond, Sheldon Gellar, Michael Horowitz, John Hunwick, Tom Kelly, David Killingray, Matt Kirwin, Murray Last, René Lemarchand, Beverly Mack, Pat Manning, Lenny Markovitz, Michael McClindon, Paul Nugent, Dov Ronen, Connie Stephens, Shawkat Toorawa, and Leo Villalón. Jeffrey Metzel, whose untimely death I describe in these pages, would certainly have related to my African horse problem.

Most of the events related in this story take place in the Republic of Niger, a country that consistently ranks dead last on the United Nations' human poverty index (HPI) and human development index (HDI). Niger has the highest infant and young child mortality rates in the world, as well as the second lowest per capita number of doctors. No other country sends fewer kids to high school; only Bhutan and Haiti send fewer to primary school. World record for highest rate of adult illiteracy? Niger. When gender inequality and political-economic opportunities for women are factored in, Niger continues to trail the global pack. The only country that at one point challenged Niger for the dubious distinction of overall underdevelopment—Sierra Leone—at least had a civil war to blame. In contrast—and except for sporadic uprisings among its Saharan Tuaregs, incited by Libya's Qadafy—Niger is uncharacteristically peaceful. It is just dirt poor.

Why do I invoke such statistics, since this book is not a primer on Niger? Only to underscore how distorted our understanding of the "Third World" becomes when we rely on simple numbers and other brute measures of misery to frame our imagination of the impoverished Other. No World Bank or United Nations indicator can reflect the underlying value that justifies a journey to Niger to settle a horse problem. In Hausa, the explanatory word is *mutumci*: dignity. If only we realized what a deficit of *mutumci* we had here in America, we might begin to emulate the poor but noble Africans who embody it.

Accordingly, the reader will note that I have not directly converted Nigerian prices into American dollars. That would have defeated one of the morals of this story—that "rational choice" cannot always be reduced to monetary value. For those who insist on knowing how much the original horse actually cost, all I can do is paraphrase Alhaji Mallam Harouna, my village host: for the amount of "cowry shells" (the literal word for money) that I "killed" to undertake this journey, I could have bought ten horses.

As always, greatest thanks go to that French West Indian lady, possibly the first Martinican woman to become Jewish since King Louis IX expelled the Jews in 1684, who is accepting enough of my *mishugas* (Yiddish: "craziness") to allow me to take our young son into the West African bush. That lady is my bride of over twenty years, Loïza Nellec-Miles.

William F. S. Miles
Seekonk, Massachusetts

GLOSSARY OF HAUSA TERMS USED IN TEXT

Note: The three Hausa "hooked"
letters b, d, k are indicated by
apostrophe: 'b,'d, k'.

ajami: Hausa written in Arabic
    script
alhaji: man who has performed
    the pilgrimage to Mecca.
    (The corresponding feminine
    singular term is hajiya.)
Alhamdu lillahi: "Praised be God"
allura: needle, medical injection
amin: amen
Anasara (pl., Anasaru): white
    person, Christian (used in
    Niger)
ba, babu: no, none
babban gida: bearer of name of
    founder of homestead
'bace: spoiled, ruined, degraded
bak'in mutum: black person
Ba komi: "It's nothing (to worry
    about)"
barantaka: patron-client
    relationship
Barka da zuwa: "Welcome"
    (lit., "Blessings on your
    coming")
Bature: white person; European
    (used in Nigeria)
boko: Western education; Roman
    script
cizo: biting
doki: horse
gado: inheritance

galadima: a royal title
gamsu: frivolous chatter while
    eating; to be pleased
gurgu: cripple
Haka fa: "It is so"
hakimi: district chief
hak'uri; Hak'uri maganin duniya:
    patience; "Patience is the
    medicine/remedy/solution for
    life"
hankali: intelligence, good sense
iska: wind; name of author's first
    horse
kamazuru: reins
keke: bicycle; wheelchair
ku'di: money; lit., cowry shells
kumya, kunya: shame
lada: commission
lafiya, lafiya lau: (in) health; all
    right
linjami: horse bit
madalla: expression of thanks or
    approval
mahaukaci (pl., mahaukata): crazy
    person
mai-gari: village chief
mallam: teacher; Islamic priest;
    mister
mantuwa: forgetfulness
masoya: those whom one loves
mukhtar: chief (Arabic)
mulhin: saddle blanket
Mun gode: "We thank you."
Musulmi: Muslim
Na gode: "I thank you"

naira: currency of Nigeria

nasara, nasaru: *See* anasara, anasaru

Ranke ya da'de: "May you live long!"

rishin hankali: stupidity; lit., lack of good sense

rumbu (pl., rumbuna): grain storage bins

sa'a: luck; name of author's third horse.

Sai Allah: "By the grace of God"

Salaam aleikum: "Peace unto you" (Arabic)

Sannu! (pl., Sannunku!): general greeting

santi: forgetfulness from eating; inappropriate behavior or comments while eating

sarki: emir, sultan, king

shari'a; shariah: law; Koranic law

Shi ke nan: "That's it, that's all"

sirdi: saddle

talauci: poverty

tashin hankali: argument, unrest

tsegumi: scandal, gossip

uwargida: senior wife, first wife

wahalla: trouble; name of author's second horse.

wayo: cunning

yeye: swaggering youth

zance: conversation

GEOGRAPHICAL REFERENCES

Abuja: capital of Nigeria

Babura: Nigerian border town

Daura: district and emirate encompassing Yardaje; also, district capital

Garke: regional market in Nigeria

Hamada: one of two Yekuwa villages

Kaduna: city of northern Nigeria with large Christian minority; former British provincial capital

Kano: major city of Northern Nigeria

Katsina: state encompassing Yardaje; also, state capital city

Kofai: one of two Yekuwa villages

Kwaya: regional market in Niger

Magaria: county encompassing Yekuwa; also, county seat where author did Peace Corps service

Maiaduwa: regional market in Nigeria

Niamey: capital of Niger

Niger: former French colony in West Africa; independent since 1960.

Nigeria: former British colony in West Africa; independent since 1960

Yardaje: Hausa village in Nigeria, near border with Niger

Yekuwa: Hausa village in Niger, near border with Nigeria

Zango: neighboring town in Nigeria to Yardaje

DRAMATIS PERSONAE

Alhaji Aminu: chief of Yekuwa-Kofai

Alhaji Habou: Fulani friend, killed when roof caved

Alhaji Harou: *See* Sarkin Fulani

Alhaji Lawal: "hygiene inspector" of Daura (traditional title); conferred on Samuel his Hausa name

Alhaji Mallam Harouna: preacher friend and author's correspondent from Yekuwa

Alhaji Moutari Aliyu Yardaje: friend who now owns a used-car import company in Kano

Alhaji Muhammadu Bashar: *See* Sarkin Daura

Andy Cook: graduate school friend and development consultant

Bill Casey ("Bill One"): Peace Corps Volunteer in Magaria who already had a horse

Brah: antagonist who claimed Sa'a as his inheritance

Dan Mallam: Passover Exodus interlocutor

Danjuma: chief of Yekuwa-Kofai to whom author first confided Sa'a

Eliyu Mai-Gemu ("The Bearded One"): Elihu Kover, friend who visited from New York City

Faralu: horse groom in Yekuwa

Galadima: adviser to the chief of Yekuwa

Hassan, son of chief of Yardaje

Iska: author's first horse; "wind"

Isma'il: Ishmael; Arabic version of Sama'ila

Jagga: town crier of Yekuwa

Jeffrey Metzel: graduate school friend and development consultant who died in air crash off West African coast

Lawali: friend and business associate during author's Peace Corps days

Lawal Nuhu (Lawali): schoolteacher resident in Yardaje; author's close friend and correspondent

Loïza: wife of author, mother of Samuel

Ma'aru Tangu: photocopy messenger

Mallam Beel: author's name in Yardaje

Mamane Alassane: author's housekeeper in Magaria

Mista Bello: author's name in Yekuwa

Murtalla Yardaje (Nigeria): relative of Souleymane (Niger)

Musa Tela: "Moses the Tailor" of Yardaje

Sa'a: author's third horse; "luck"

Sama'ila: Hausa name given to author's son

Sarkin Daura: emir of Daura, the emirate in Nigeria encompassing Yardaje

Sarkin Fulani ("King of the Fulanis") Harou: chief of Yardaje and surrounding villages

Sarkin Magaria Harou: chief of Magaria, the district in Niger encompassing Yekuwa.

Sarkin Makaho: chief of the Blind

Sidi: village vaccinator; "Needle-Man"

Souleymane Abba: Islamic preacher friend from Magaria

Sultan of Zinder (Damagaram) one of seven high chiefs of Niger, in the province encompassing Yekuwa

Usman Kongo: proverbialist of Yardaje

Wahalla: author's second horse; "trouble"

MY AFRICAN HORSE PROBLEM

1

You're home after work, sitting comfortably in the living room, and going through the day's postal harvest. Bills, advertisements, the usual "special fourth class" (i.e., junk) mail: you flip through them semi-consciously, wondering what you'll have for dinner, what program you'll watch that evening. And then you come upon that letter whose handwriting, return address, or canceled stamp rivets you. Even before breaking the seal, you are transported deep into the past, back into those dimly recalled days before you had kids, before you were married, before you landed that job that so defines who you are today.

It could be from an old lover, newly divorced or widowed, discreetly inquiring about your own marital and romantic status. It could be from that former chum with whom you'd had a falling out—you've long since forgotten why—seeking reconciliation before the recently diagnosed cancer runs its course. Or the letter could be from a black Muslim priest you'd befriended sixteen years before but hadn't seen since, informing you about the death of the village chief and the resulting inheritance dispute surrounding your horse—or *was* it your horse?—that more than a decade prior you'd left deep in the African bush.

That was the letter I found myself staring at. And that's the simple explanation why I was now on a Royal Dutch Airlines flight bound for Kano, Nigeria, the horse's proper heir—my ten-year-old son Samuel—fidgeting excitedly beside me.

Sa'a was a gorgeous dark brown stallion, swift but obedient, whom in 1986 I'd purchased in a Nigerian horse market thanks to Ted Kennedy. True, Senator Kennedy didn't exactly sponsor the horse trading, but his office did intervene when research materials I'd sent through the diplomatic pouch in 1984 were lost en route to Washington. Not only were my two hundred painstakingly completed questionnaires gone, but dashed forever were my Mission Impossible images of the foreign service courier handcuffed to—or at least safeguarding with his life—the contents of the confidential and mysterious "pouch." My cardboard boxes arrived broken and emptied of survey sheets. With Kennedy's support, my government research grant was reactivated so that I could return to Nigeria in the summer of 1986 and redo the surveys in the same backcountry Hausa villages where I'd already spent twelve months in 1983–84.

Hausaland is an indistinct swath of territory spanning most of northern Nigeria and a good part of its northern neighbor, the Republic of Niger. Just south of the Sahara, the land is sandy and parched, the people subsisting on millet and sorghum grown during the miraculous three months of the year that—"if Allah is willing"—it rains. Overwhelmingly Muslim, but with undertones of pre-Islamic animism and sorcery, the black African Hausa are indefatigable farmers and tireless traders. They live in symbiotic harmony with the "red-skinned" Fulani, some of whose ancestors conquered Hausaland in the early nineteenth century and most of whom, nomads still, tend the cattle, goats, and sheep that graze relentlessly upon the dry, brown, fragile Sahelian ground. It was from one of these more affluent Fulani that I had purchased my equestrian grail.

Actually, it was a re-purchase. After I'd taken the sleek quadruped for a trial ride (not a local custom but a concession granted to the White Man used to test drives in metaphorically horse-powered modes of conveyance), and while I was negotiating an equitable price under an enormous baobab, on the other side of the tree the well-endowed Fulani was buying the prize animal right out from under me. The frustration, due in part to my own dilatory negotiating tactics—and this, after stressful hours of uninformed horse examinations under the scorching sub-Saharan sun—almost reduced me to tears. Mustering every ounce of crosscultural persuasiveness, I appealed vociferously to the "King of the Horsetraders"—such sales are conducted strictly through designated professional intermediaries. The King of the Horsetraders in turn prevailed upon the compassionate Fulani to sell me back the horse, at cost. Was it the strange sight of a Hausa-speaking White Man sweating hard in a pulsing bush market, visibly upset over a horse transaction gone awry, that touched the mild nomad? This I cannot affirm. I can only aver that I paid the Fulani his horse money, gave the King of the Horsetraders his commission, and tipped an on-looker the requisite "witness gratuity." For the "Luck" it took to acquire him I immediately named my new horse Sa'a.

I also began to think that, henceforth, I should cease this stressful habit of buying and selling endearing horses in Hausaland.

Sa'a was the third horse I'd owned in Africa. The previous one, Wahalla, well deserved his Hausa name—"Trouble." Wahalla, whom I'd bought in 1983, had the annoying habit of sneaking away. It was bad enough when he slunk away from my compound in the village. But when he escaped from his tether in the bush it created quite some trouble, for how do you catch a runaway horse in the empty expanses of the Sahel? Only by relying on the kindness of strangers—unknown Africans, all—who always managed to corral my wanton Wahalla.

It is to Wahalla, in fact, that my mind drifts when I catalog the most embarrassing moments of my life. After one of his periodic escapes from the seemingly empty bush to which I periodically withdrew for solitude, Wahalla was caught by a roving farmer far from the saddle and stirrups that I had removed so that the ungrateful beast could repose comfortably. Out of nowhere a small crowd appeared to watch earnestly as I remounted my barebacked steed, only to see me overestimate the jump needed to get back on top and tumble ignominiously to the ground on Wahalla's other side. After reassuring themselves that I was not hurt—and perhaps that this was not just another of the crazy White Man's customs—they allowed themselves the kind of laughter that had once filled Western audiences at similar antics performed by the likes of Buster Keaton and Charlie Chaplin.

In his defense I should acknowledge that Wahalla was oversexed. Usually he kept fleeing to pursue female company: his urge to reproduce was enormous, as was his instrument for satisfying the urge. Were you ever embarrassed by the extended member of your pet? When my girlfriend ventured across the Atlantic and into the African bush to check up on the strange man still courting her from afar, I was. When my *equus* stirred, even *homo sapiens*—of both genders—had to take note.

Sa'a, on the other hand, was to inflict the opposite kind of embarrassment. Agreeing to stud him out with the mare of another villager—and accepting the customary payment in advance—I had failed to predetermine his sexual maturity. During an excruciating forty-five minutes out on the edge of the village, we watched as Sa'a suspiciously eyed his maiden date and took only a few awkward, inadequate steps to satisfy her and her prepaid master. Maybe he was just painfully shy: after all, even if he had been previously deflowered, having to perform in public may have crimped his style. Or so I ridiculously reasoned, as if I were not merely the owner of a sexually immature horse but the parent of a woefully uninformed adolescent. So ashamed was I of Sa'a's virile ignorance that I offered to return the stud money. But the mare's owner declined: in Hausaland, non-consummation is no grounds for refund.

Before Sa'a, then, there was Wahalla, and before Wahalla, Iska, my very first African horse. Owning and galloping on Iska—so-called because he was said to run as fast as the "Wind"—had been one of the formative experiences of my life as a Peace Corps Volunteer in Niger in the late 1970s. Yet on my own, it would never have occurred to me to own a horse in Hausaland. For this I am eternally grateful to another Peace Corps Volunteer (PCV), William Casey of Louisiana.

During Peace Corps training in Niamey, the capital of Niger, we trainees were joined by seasoned Volunteers. Even those with only one year of service behind them appeared as strange but superior beings. We looked like pale Americans; they were sun-scorched and in Africanized dress. We spoke English and practiced a collegiate version of Molière's tongue; they knew Hausa or Zarma and African-accented French. We were hyper about being in Niger; they were supremely laid back. Yet even among these generic cultural hybrids one or two stood out as particular space cadets. Bill Casey was one of them.

Bill, a balding twenty-something of slight build and medium height, spoke slowly, his speech decelerated to the unhurried rhythm of African bush life. His communications sounded tentative, as if behind every sentence lurked a major qualification or an outrageous joke. Gradually regaling me with the virtues of Magaria, the town where he was posted as an English teacher, Bill succeeded in tempering my Peace Corps machismo, a naive bias with which a number of us male Volunteers were greatly afflicted: the puerile belief that the toughest and therefore most authentic transcultural experience went to him who secured the most geographically remote posting, one where there was also no other Anasara (white person) around. Befriending Bill, I was torn between applying for Nguigmui—the ultimate outer limits post, somewhere near Lake Chad—and Magaria. Friendship won out over machismo and, for the townsfolk for whom all whites looked alike, forced us to modify our local names: he became Bill Daya (Bill The First) and I, Bill Biyu (Bill Number Two).

Part of Bill's appeal lay in his horse ownership. Like me, he didn't have much of a pre–Peace Corps history of equestrianism: occasional pony rides in childhood, some horseback riding at summer camp. Becoming an overnight horse owner—even while learning to be an English teacher in Africa—required an outright redefinition of self, a willingness to assume yet another vaguely imaginable role. More than I had appreciated, Bill

Casey was musing way out of the typical American kid's box. When we went riding together in the flat sandy plains outside Magaria, rather than imagining us as Buffalo Bill cowboys herding out on the open range, Bill would invoke Genghis Khan and his horse-mounted hordes marauding across the steppes of Mongolia.

Bill initiated me, a flatfoot from Long Island, into the wild idea of owning a horse in Hausaland. But without Mamane Alassane, I wouldn't have had the slightest idea of how to actually care for Iska. In fact, without Mamane I wouldn't have known much about anything in Hausaland.

In local parlance, Mamane was my *boy*. It sounds pejorative, of course, the very word a direct consequence of colonialism and the enduring legacies of racism and imperialism. Would it be less shocking to describe him as my "manservant," "domestic," or "butler"? But *boy* is what he—and all Africans working for Peace Corps Volunteers in this part of the continent—was indeed called in Hausa, French, and English. However antithetical to core American and Peace Corps values, deep-seated social divisions based on poverty, wealth, and piety made it impossible to escape completely colonial and postcolonial role expectations and the language that reinforces them.

Not that hierarchical relationships were an innovation of colonialism. Indigenous Hausa society is anything but egalitarian, much better understood in terms of hierarchy than democracy. Social scientists use "patron-client" relations to describe this world-wide phenomenon; in Francophone Africa, even mere Peace Corps Volunteers are typically called *patron*, the French word for "boss." If you look up the word *bara* in a Hausa dictionary, you will find "slave" as a common translation. But nowadays *bara* is much closer to *boy*, the subordinate in a patron-client relationship.

Such a relationship cuts both ways. A patron is required to look after his client, and in return the client is expected to provide various services for his patron. Understanding the boundaries of these expectations is one of the most difficult things for an outsider to apprehend, along with the virtual impossibility of recreating American-style friendships across African patron-client lines. Still, a few words to defend the seeming incongruity of young Peace Corps Volunteers employing personal care attendants are in order.

Mamane came with the house. It sounds crass, but no sooner had the Peace Corps Land Rover dropped me off at my modest but Western-style home in Magaria—Bill Casey was away vacationing, so I was alone—then Mamane appeared. Extremely dark-skinned with fine facial features, of indeterminate age but certainly my elder, soft-spoken but far from obsequious, Mamane took it for granted that he would be my *boy*: he had worked for previous Peace Corps Volunteers at the same house, spoke sufficient French, and was eminently acquainted with Anasara idiosyncrasies. We never discussed *whether* he would work for me, or under what terms—I merely asked what his previous salary had been. Thus, with nary a written reference or formal interview, I took on this absolute stranger to be my constant companion, language instructor, house cleaner, launderer, dish washer, handy man, market shopper, messenger, and—after acquiring Iska—horse groom. For these services I paid Mamane the equivalent of 10 percent of my own monthly living allowance of $250.00.

Was this exploitation? It was the only possible employment Mamane could have secured, and it elevated him, in status as well as wealth, well above the ranks of the wageless subsistence farmers and petty tradesmen who otherwise populated Magaria. In the absence of the machines that perform so many of our household tasks in America, Mamane's service liberated me to perform the tasks for which I'd been brought to Niger in the first place: preparing lesson plans, teaching, grading, tutoring. Years later, first when one "egalitarian" PCV refused to employ a *boy* on principle (or from stinginess), and then when Peace Corps pulled out of Magaria entirely, Mamane's finances took a steep dive.

Mamane knew not only how to take care of horses but also how to track them. Some few months before I was to return to America I lost the only key to the house. I had been out in the bush riding Iska and, dismounting to pass water, unwittingly allowed the key to fall from my pocket. Only upon returning to the house did I realize what had happened. Knowing that there was no locksmith in the town, and that the only way to enter my home would be to break an expensive glass door pane—and that there were no glaziers in town to replace that, either—I nearly panicked. Nonplussed, Mamane volunteered to follow Iska's hoof prints back out into the bush—no easy task, considering that the sand also contained the tracks of countless other horses, donkeys, oxen, and bipeds. We returned into the empty countryside—he walking ahead, myself ignominiously atop Iska—Mamane assiduously tracking prints that were to me barely visible. Eventually we arrived at a little patch in the parched Sahelian soil that, hours after I'd urinated there, still showed unmistakable signs of dampness. Sure enough, sifting through the sand between the urine spot and my own prints near Iska's, dusk nearly upon us, Mamane recovered the house key.

But it was not Mamane's tracking abilities that impressed me most. It was rather his patience and piety, and his matter-of-fact faith.

God is commonly invoked in Hausa conversation. "With the will of Allah," "only Allah," "Allah is great" habitually punctuates even the most mundane of dialogues. But Mamane's enthusiastic way of invoking the divine made it sound as if God were a close but powerful friend, just around the corner, constantly taking care of us even if he was too busy to appear in person.

Mamane lived his life knowing that Allah would make sure that everything worked out in the end: being patient was not just a virtue but an expression of faith. "Patience is the medicine of life" was the first Hausa proverb that Mamane taught, and it came rather early in his tutoring of me.

For it was Mamane who really taught me to speak Hausa. When I first arrived in Magaria, I had had the benefit of a couple of weeks of excellent Peace Corps language training. But that was just enough to master some of the innumerable greetings and to scrape by in the marketplace. Mamane spoke much better French than I did Hausa; in fact, as far as I was concerned, he was fluent.

From the outset I let Mamane know that I wanted to speak Hausa, and he patiently tutored me, word by word. The daily proportional balance between French and Hausa slowly shifted, and I distinctly recall the euphoria I felt, three months after arrival, when we had gone for an entire day without once speaking French. We never went back—except for the one time I unfairly chewed him out, entirely in French, for having let a relative of the landlord stay in the house during my extended summer absence.

Except for my occasional departures from Magaria, I saw Mamane virtually every day of my two years as a Peace Corps Volunteer. The question of "days off" never arose; he set the work conditions, not I. He who called me *mai-gida* (the Hausa equivalent of *patron*) changed me much more than I changed him. In slightly modified form, that is what you will hear every Peace Corps Volunteer admit—that our host site changed us more than we changed it. Mamane's imprint on my soul is, to a large degree, my Peace Corps experience.

Mamane's wife Ladi was an animated beauty, not at all shy when speaking to Anasaru or anyone else. Without being outwardly affectionate (a cultural taboo) theirs was the closest I ever observed to a loving marriage, based on mutual respect, akin to what we expect in the West. Though divorce is commonplace in Hausa society—at least as common as polygamy—Mamane and Ladi remained together, no co-wife complicating the relationship, for over three decades.

"Patience is the medicine of life." Exactly thirty years after I first met Mamane in 1977, I broke down when, on my arrival in Magaria, a mutual friend informed that Mamane had died only three days earlier. It is not seemly for a man to shed tears in Hausaland, but I did so. "Patience," my friend counseled me, patting my shoulder. "Be patient."

It was painful disposing of Iska. But when my two-year stint as Volunteer was winding down, I had no choice. An elderly *ancien combattant*—a war veteran, one of the thousands of black Africans who had fought for France in Europe during World War II—made me an offer and tendered a down payment. But his monthly *mandat*, his money order pension from France, "mysteriously" kept not arriving; two days before I was to depart, the crafty old warrior was still short by half. Although stressed out, I wasn't the least surprised. The next day I dispatched Mamane to a distant market, hoping he'd land a buyer. He did—but the grimy bundle of faded French West African francs for which he'd exchanged Iska imparted a great deal more reproachful pain than pecuniary pleasure.

There was no professional need for me to own Iska. School was an eight-minute walk from my Peace Corps home, and no self-respecting teacher in Niger would ride a horse to work, anyway. I bought that first horse in Africa strictly as a pastime, influenced by Bill Casey (who finished his two years of service when I was half-way into mine). Only in retrospect did I recognize the acute psychological utility, as a solitary White Man, of riding in Hausaland. Its importance, in terms of mental health, was even keener when I would later own Wahalla, and then Sa'a. In short, horse riding was my antidote to sociocultural claustrophobia.

What is the allure of West Africa for the sojourning Westerner? There one finds a society in which people are regarded foremost not as potential customers, as in our own, but as fellow human beings; a culture where person-to-person contact is primary; communities where everyone knows everyone, and genuinely cares about each other's health and welfare. On a daily level, this translates into long, repetitive, ritualized greetings that begin the moment one leaves one's home: "How did you sleep? Did you awake in health? How fares the household? How are you standing the heat/the cold? How is your first wife?" (the Hausa are polygamous). "How are the children? How is the work going? What is your level of fatigue? How do you see the state of the world?" Most questions can be answered by a simple *lafiya lau!*—"in health"—though variation with "Praise be to Allah!" is also perfectly acceptable. To "How goes the work?" you reply, "Thankful for it" and with regards to fatigue—well, you never state you have any. For the American raised on the cursory "Hi" or "Howya doin'?" African salutations constitute etiquette shock.

And if you are what the Hausa call either an Anasara (literally, Christian) or Bature (literally, European)—that is, a White Man, for all whites are automatically regarded here as Christian and European—and you speak any of their language, then you'll be asked to greet all the more. For you are a phenomenon: a rich foreigner, an emissary from the white world, who has bothered to learn the local tongue. You will be followed down the street, Pied Piper–like, by children chanting, in a combination of Hausa and French, "White Man! White Man! Give me a gift!" Some adults, too, will call out to you by your skin color or presumed religion. You know they mean no harm, that no insult is intended; but after six months, after twelve months, after a year and a half of residence, you think it long overdue that they call you by your name rather than your race.

If you have studied the history or sociology of colonialism before winding up here, you may know that Europeans imposed a skin color hierarchy on societies that were already highly stratified, but not by race. Colonialism made it easy to transpose the basis of superiority to skin color, and independence alone could not erase this skin-based superiority bias. But if you have not had the benefit of such higher education, you may assume that a hierarchy based on skin color differences is somehow universal. And it will be harder for you to think outside of your own skin.

When you can't take this perverse celebrity anymore—when even buying eggs in the marketplace becomes a complex exercise in multicultural diplomacy, crowd control, and racial stress management—you retreat into your home. You stay inside to preserve your privacy—a concept that is totally lacking in the cultural environs—but the kids start banging on your door, or pitching pebbles, to get your attention. After a spell of this, your house begins to feel like a prison. Outside, relentless stardom; inside, stir-crazed entrapment.

So you saddle up your horse and you trot out of town. On horseback, nobody expects you to halt for all the customary greetings: you can just wave and go! Even the kids tire of running after you, once you canter outside the town limits. Then, following a sandy track into the empty bush, you break into a gallop! You are thrilled by the combination of speed and rolling rhythm, by the thump-tikatik-thump on the soft Sahelian sand, by the slight danger of a stumble or a fall, by the sheer magnificence of racing alone, on your own horse, out in this vast African savannah. You are alone. You are free! You take your horse back down to a canter, and then down to a brisk walk. Over his heavy breathing you can now hear the occasional braying of distant donkeys, the bellowing of cattle, and the bleating of sheep and goats. Sometimes the hot wind carries the sound of distant women pounding millet in huge mortars with their wooden pestles. The sun begins to turn orange on the horizon and a hoot-hoot-hoot joins the improvised score of the bush. You follow the sound: an exotic bird with a long, curved, bright red bill swoops into its baobab tree, preparing to nest for the night. You are alone, you are free . . . and when you finally return to town, in a final gallop on the home stretch, triumphantly answering the calls of "How's the horse? How was the galloping?" with "See him here! We galloped in health!" your soul has been restored, your cultural claustrophobia assuaged, and your love for living in Hausaland totally reinvigorated.

While I did not need Iska to work as a Peace Corps teacher in Magaria, my research as a Fulbright scholar in 1983 did require a horse. For the only way to travel between Yardaje and Yekuwa, the two villages that I was comparing, was either by foot or on horseback. Yekuwa villagers thought little of making the sixteen-mile round trip by "the motorcar Allah has issued us"—that is, by legging it—just to attend Yardaje's weekly market. For a White Man of my stature and stamina, though, a horse was definitely required.

Even by Nigerian standards, Yardaje is poor. Most people live in square mud huts, with mud-and-thatch roofs that must be reinforced before the annual rainy season to prevent leakage. Some wealthier inhabitants have built cement huts with aluminum "pan" roofs. There is no electricity, no indoor plumbing or running water. Hand-cranked pumps and open wells supply waters of various tints; kerosene lamps and flashlights offer specks of illumination after dark. Still, viewed from Yekuwa—with its grass (instead of mud) huts, ubiquitous donkeys, and comparative lack of commerce—Yardaje, with its dozens of bicycles and motorcycles (not to mention the chief's own Peugeot), seems like a bustling, cosmopolitan town. In each of these nondescript villages there live a few thousand souls.

Colonial records indicate that both settlements are about a century old (1809 for Yardaje, some years before that for Yekuwa). Oral history evokes a much older genesis. The settlements have experienced conquest and grandeur, decay and restoration, factionalism and civic pride. Yekuwa, having once splintered into rival camps, is actually two villages, Yekuwa-Kofai and Yekuwa-Hamada, which through natural growth have gradually re-merged into each other; to the uninformed eye, they look like a single settlement. But there are still two chiefs. My own participation in these communities is but a blip in a much longer story of life in rural Hausaland.

In both villages, the vibrancy of life belies the reality of poverty. In terms of personal possessions, not even a chief may own as much as I pack into a suitcase for even a couple of weeks' visit. "You have lots of baggage," Alhaji Aminu observes matter-of-factly, and I am indeed embarrassed. There is no village bank: excess income is typically invested in livestock, not savings accounts. And goats do get lost, cows do get sick . . . One close associate, whom I shall not identify in deference to the intimacy of the request, once humbly asked if I would supply him with *diraw*—a word that I had never heard before, and which took me some time to figure out was actually more English than Hausa. Derived from the British usage of "drawer," M. was asking me for underwear. Until then, it never occurred to me what bounty, in the right context, a wrapped package of Fruit of the Loom could mean.

It all depends on the rains . . . A good rainy season used to be able to assure a satisfactory harvest of food crops until the next. Now, even that is not so sure. Throughout Hausaland, seasonal hunger is common for many families in the months that overlap the emptying of last season's granaries and their filling from the current one. Sanitation is barely understood: in Yekuwa, I was told, my latrine was the first one ever dug in the village, the open fields being the customary site for relieving oneself. Viewed from a Western perspective, poverty in the Third World means uncertainty: of income, of health, of the future. It is a situation that, for us on the wealthy side of the planet, demands urgent remedy. But for the Hausa, *talauci* is more or less a permanent condition, one that is endured with the help of God: *sai Allah*, you often hear as a code of solace in otherwise desperate situations. And since Allah enjoins believers to help those less fortunate, begging is a reputable profession. Not lucrative, but honorable.

Yet for all these grim material realities, there is a sense of solidarity and purpose, an exuberance, that pulses throughout the rural Hausa village. In Haiti, which is statistically better off than Nigeria and Niger (its GDP per capita is more than that of both countries combined), the local term that encapsulates the struggle for existence is *misère*. That is a defeatist mind frame that you rarely encounter in Hausaland.

"Commuting" by horse between Yekuwa and Yardaje, through the empty bush and usually alone, typified my existence for the better part of a year. And why had I decided to traipse between them in the first place? In a nutshell, because some rather presumptuous Europeans had drawn an invisible line between the two settlements seventy-five years before. As a result, Yekuwa, in the same county where I had previously taught English with the Peace Corps, was in Niger; neighboring Yardaje, however, lay in a different country entirely: the Federal Republic of Nigeria.

Students of Africa are well acquainted with the notorious 1884–85 Treaty of Berlin and the ensuing "Scramble for Africa" which legitimized European colonization of the "Dark Continent." Oblivious to, or uninterested in, the indigenous peoples who populated their newly declared field of conquest, White Men in Europe drew boundary lines that would forever separate Black Folk in Africa. One of these many arbitrary lines cut through territory populated mainly by speakers of the Hausa language. On one side of this superimposed border, established between 1906 and 1908, the Hausa found themselves under British overlords in Nigeria; on the other side, in Niger, their cousins discovered that they were colonized by the French. Both colonies became independent in 1960. Their boundary lines, however, remained intact.

Fresh out of college in 1977, I was far from being one of those "students of Africa . . . well acquainted" with the Treaty of Berlin and the Scramble for Africa: I didn't even know that there *was* a country named Niger! When the Peace Corps recruiter informed me over the phone one Friday

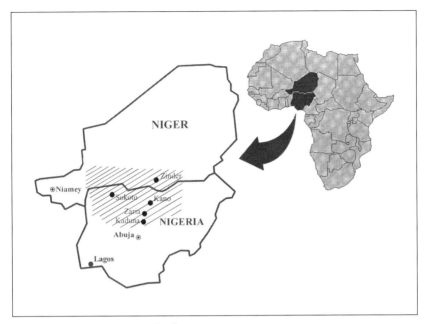

Approximate range of Hausaland.

afternoon during my senior year at Vassar that there were slots open for English teachers in Zaïre and Niger, and that I had until Monday to choose between them, I blithely assumed that Niger was the capital of Nigeria. (As for Zaïre, over that same weekend a civil war broke out—again—in the ever-simmering province of Shaba. While I was still tempted—for it was truly in the "heart of Africa"—moving to Zaïre would have been a harder sell to Mom.)

Today, of course, no country still calls itself Zaïre (but there is a so-called Democratic Republic of the Congo), and Nigeria has acquired an almost fearful reputation for oil-driven extravagance and corruption. It is the fifth largest supplier of petroleum to the United States; the most populous country in all Africa; and a regional player in conflicts (and their resolution), both civil and international, throughout the continent. Although many of its citizens (including the ones in the oil-rich sectors) live in abject poverty, Nigeria is an African powerhouse. Its elections make a mockery of the expression "free and fair," but its transition to a democratic form of government mesmerizes students of its intricate politics.

Besides sharing a border and the first five letters of its name, what does Niger have in common with Nigeria? Niger does possess one precious mineral—uranium—but its multinational exploitation, and the restricted market for it, have not permitted anywhere near the kind of largess that oil has for Nigeria. Indeed, ever since the United Nations began in 1990 to rank countries according to their wealth, literacy, and longevity, Niger has consistently come in last. This, in a country that has—episodic rebellions by Tuareg warrior nomads notwithstanding—enjoyed relative peace and stability.

In addition to the Tuareg (proud desert dwellers related to the Berbers of North Africa), Niger has herding peoples known as Kanuri, Tubu, and Fulani. But the two groups that make up almost three-quarters of the entire population (now about 12 million, over 90 percent of whom are Muslim) are farmers: the Zarma and the Hausa. Under French colonialism, the Zarma developed a secondary specialization: soldiering. The Hausa, who make up about half of the country, have long cherished trading as their non-agricultural specialization.

Nigeria (over 120 million inhabitants, about half of whom are Muslim) is also about half Hausa—or at least Hausa-speaking, so expansive is this West African lingua franca. (For some reason, Swahili has always enjoyed greater public recognition among Americans, even though Hausaphones outnumber Swahili-speakers.) But rather than being first among about half a dozen peoples, as in Niger, the Hausa in Nigeria are paramount (especially if agglomerated with their urban, hyphenated Hausa-Fulani counterparts) among at least 250 ethnic groupings. Two major demographic rivals are the Yoruba, in the southwest, and the Igbo (who launched the ill-fated Biafra war of secession in the 1960s) in the southeast.

Southern Nigeria, where the Yoruba and Igbo predominate, is green from tropical rain forest and coastal waterings. Northern Nigeria, homeland to the Hausa, is dry, dusty, and windswept. In this it resembles most of Niger—or at least the populated regions of that country, most of whose people dwell in the sandy Sahel. (North of the Sahel, encompassing most of Niger's land mass, is the Sahara.) For eight hundred miles an arbitrary, geometric, mostly invisible line calculated by European empire framers over a century ago cuts through these sandy African flatlands declaring: "This side is Nigeria! That side is Niger."

However artificial the initial demarcation, the border has taken on a life of its own. Even remote dwellers along the borderline—*especially* dwellers along the borderline—know full well exactly where the line cuts. More important, they know that they belong to one side or the other, one country or the other, either to Niger or to Nigeria. This is so even when they share an otherwise identical profile as Muslim Hausa farmers.

Although their day-to-day lives may not appear so different to the casual observer, the Hausa borderliners do harbor a strong sense of their side of the divide. Though far from teeming, chaotic, and dangerous Lagos, at the completely opposite end of Nigeria's north-side transversal, the villagers of Yardaje cannot shake the association with their country's megacity. And these same villagers look down, however patronizingly, on their country cousins across the border in Niger. In Yardaje, I have written elsewhere

> a brashness, an assertiveness, contrasts sharply with the humility, deference, and reserve that characterize Yekuwa [in Niger]. Yardaj[e] men are aggressive where Yekuwa men are submissive; they are animated where 'yan Yekuwa are passive. The contrast in village character is even more striking among women. 'Yar Yardaj[e] are more direct, more extroverted, more jocose than 'yar Yekuwa. Rarely did women and girls in Yekuwa treat me to the good-natured teasing and half-serious marriage propositions that made living in Yardaj[e] such a harrowing delight! (*Hausaland Divided*, p. 301)

Such are the quotidian consequences of having been arbitrarily separated by a once-colonial, now-international boundary. Differences in educational policies, official language use, economic prospects, military-civilian relations, role of chiefs, religious practices—all these filter down to remote communities along the borderline. National stereotypes—individualism and cockiness in Nigeria, collectivism and self-effacement in Niger—find their equivalents in these otherwise similar neighboring communities. "In Yardaj[e] one finds tolerance for government and affinity with traditional authority. In Yekuwa," I noted twenty years ago, "one finds fear of . . . authority outside the village."

Imagery based on the head best represents the difference between Niger and Nigeria, as experienced where the two countries meet. A villager in Yekuwa said that those on the other side, in Nigerian Yardaje, "feel their head"—that is, are arrogant. In contrast, my friend Hassan—son of the chief of Yardaje, faithful breakfast companion, and renowned "Cattle King"—put an index finger to each of his temples to demonstrate the character of the people of Yekuwa/Niger. Bowing slightly, he then swayed slowly, giving a faithful rendition of a pliant, submissive bull.

It would take many months of living in off-the-road borderline villages, following reams of reading and grant proposal writing, before I came to these findings. But my initial interest in exploring the Niger-Nigeria Hausa borderland—in a manner that required horse ownership—stemmed not from any academic interest or scholarly background. It rather grew out of the happenstance that placed me for two years in a medium-sized Nigérien town on a well-traveled road leading to Nigeria. The trigger, though, was a treacherous occurrence of traumatic proportions that occurred toward the end of my Peace Corps service: the house break-in and theft of my precious short-wave radio, a parting gift from my late father and my sanity-saving link to the outside world. The whole problem stemmed from an ox deal gone awry.

2

Slight in build, Lawali's limbs would strain with the effort to subdue an uncooperative bull. At other times, under the weight of a fifty-pound sack of millet perched on his head, his neck muscles would bulge frighteningly. He had the broad, flat nose so common to Africans just south of the Sahara; a general openness in his features engendered feelings of trust and sympathy. Despite his approximate twenty-seven years of age (birth records are practically unknown in this part of the world), he looked a mere adolescent.

But how could we be friends? To a middle-class American college graduate, how could a word, no matter how faithfully translated, have the same meaning as for an impoverished African oxcart driver? I should have sensed a problem when Lawali asked me not if I were his *aboki* (Hausa for "friend") but rather his *uba* ("father"). The biological absurdity of the question blinded me to what Lawali was himself wondering: could a White Man (read "rich man") ever be the equal, the peer, of a poor peasant? In a culture dominated more by the ethos of duty, obligation, and hierarchy than by equality, mutual respect, and democracy, how could my American Peace Corps ideal of international friendship make any sense? Lawali's asking if I were his father, not his friend, was a way of probing not my feelings but my responsibility for him. Such a paternalistic role could have fit either the African spirit of the village chief or the French model of the colonial *patron*.

I mentioned that Lawali was an oxcart driver. This is not entirely correct, for Lawali lacked an ox. (As it turned out, he did not own a cart, either.) After a year's acquaintance, during which he taught me the finer points of Hausa and I tried to describe far-off *Amirik*, Lawali, as subtly as he could, pitched me a business proposition. Seated on a tattered living room couch in my modest-for-America, extravagant-for-Africa abode, he was sipping a grenadine *sirop*, a non-carbonated soft drink to which, after my initial offering long before, he had taken an enduring liking. Behind me, cluttering a worktable, were piles of schoolbooks, exotic novelties like dental floss, and my precious short-wave radio/cassette player. This last item provided home-chosen music for the soul and was my sole news link to the outside world. Without exaggeration, this machine was an important anchor to my sanity.

"It's too bad I don't have my own ox," Lawali offered, out of the blue. "If I only had my own ox, I could make a lot of money."

The silence which followed was not unusual. Tropical heat, I had long since learned, slows down speech as well as movement. In Africa, there is no need to constantly fill the air with words. Silence is part of communion, of communication.

"How much do oxen go for these days?" I eventually queried.

Lawali brightened. "Beel, I know a Fulani"—a nomadic herdsman—"in the bush who wants to sell his ox. He wants only thirty thousand francs!"

Thirty thousand francs, the equivalent of approximately one hundred and fifty dollars, is a small fortune in Niger. Still, for an ox, it seemed like a reasonable price. After another minute of torpid reflection, I made my fateful offer.

"Lawali," I began, "what if I were to lend you the money for an ox? How long would it take you to pay me back the thirty thousand francs?"

Lawali was ecstatic, the more so for the success of his negotiating coup.

"Three months, Beel. Four months at the most. Every day I would work, hauling brick mud, hay, anything. Every day I would put money away to pay you back. You would have your money and I could keep the ox. All right?"

Overcoming heat-induced lethargy, I calculated. There remained nine months in my two-year Peace Corps stint. Making generous allowance for Tropical Time (in which "right away" can mean "later," "tomorrow," or "never"), I still believed that, even working at a modest clip, Lawali could fully reimburse me in time.

Beyond the money question, it was a moral issue. Here I could help out a friend and give him a real chance to succeed. I could make a personal contribution to the then fashionable Basic Human Needs strategy, the latest Peace Corps buzz term. Teaching English in a French-language school in a district capital to future Nigérien bureaucrats had never quite corresponded to my pre-induction image of helping the "poorest of the poor." Was it not for such an opportunity that I had joined the Peace Corps in the first place, to make a real difference in the lives of the impoverished? Was it not such humanitarian action that vindicated the toll in frustration and solitude that two years of teaching high school in West Africa inevitably takes?

I retrieved my not-so-cleverly concealed shoe box, counted out thirty thousand French West African francs, and handed them over to a very somber Lawali.

"Now if for any reason you don't earn enough money, Lawali, you realize we'll have to sell the ox before I leave."

"Oh, for sure, Beel, but don't worry about that," Lawali quickened. "I'll pay you back. All of it. You'll see!"

Several days later Lawali arrived at my sandy homestead smiling broadly and leading a rather small bovine by a cord which he personally had hooked through the animal's nose. The coloring, a brownish-red, gave the beast his Hausa name: Bange. For an adolescent ox, Bange was good-tempered and reliable.

Mamane, my housekeeper, did not trust Lawali. Souleymane, my handicapped imamic friend, assured me that I had done a good deed. Connie, a roving doctoral student from Wisconsin, warned me that I should not count on seeing my money again.

But I had faith. I trusted Lawali. It was a matter of friendship. Even if the oxcart business did not immediately bring in any money, I could always invoke my favorite Hausa proverb, the one that Mamane taught me: "Patience is the medicine of life." Lawali would pull through eventually. I was sure of it.

Six months later, my proverbial patience was running out. Lawali had yet to bring me a single franc. He always seemed to be busy, although not at work. Nor was he any longer available to sip *sirop* at my house.

One evening I tracked him down. "Where were you today, Lawali?"

"My cousin's daughter died, Beel, and I had to go to the funeral this morning. It was very far away and by the time I got back it was too hot for Bange to work."

"What about yesterday?" I persisted.

"Oh, yesterday was the naming ceremony for my sister's newborn baby. I couldn't miss that, could I, Beel?"

No, I conceded, Lawali could not be expected to miss his nephew's naming ceremony. "Well," I consoled myself, "we'll get right back to work tomorrow. Won't we, Lawali?"

"Gee, I'd love to, Beel, but you know my best friend is getting married tomorrow . . . Oh, you're probably worried about the money. I can tell. Don't worry, I'll get it. I told you I would, didn't I?" And Lawali sauntered home—to feed Bange, he assured me.

For an incredibly long time I deluded myself into thinking that the special occasions demanding Lawali's presence would pass soon enough and that he would finally get down to oxcart driving. Only gradually did I realize that births, deaths, and weddings would always provide Lawali a pretext not to work. When only two months remained before my return to the States, I finally confronted him and reminded him of our initial agreement.

Lawali could not accept that I might actually take Bange away from him. He loved Bange, he said. He himself would fast so that Bange might eat. He could not bear the idea of separation, he lamented. He even claimed to dream about Bange.

My volition wavered. Why not let Lawali keep the beast? Thirty thousand francs would not ruin me financially. Now I had a chance to commit an act of unmitigated generosity, a deed of pure selflessness. After all, doesn't one make sacrifices for friends?

But how many times, I reminded myself, had I condemned this very scenario—coughing up charity in the name of "developmental assistance." All of us erstwhile do-gooders coming to Africa learned what it engendered: an expectation of, followed by dependence on, the generosity of the White Man—the Provider, the Giver, the "Donor." A little liberal guilt and Whitey would fork it over.

I refused to contribute to such misconceived philanthropy. I would not be taken advantage of. I would not be a postcolonial patsy.

Forgiving the ox debt raised other, more immediate dilemmas. Were I to give Lawali Bange, would I then have to leave Mamane my horse? To begin dispersing my meager estate and Peace Corps living allowance in such a manner would touch off an untenable spiral of rising expectations.

"No," I told Lawali. "I know how you feel about Bange, but a deal is a deal. We'll have to sell him. Next market day."

"OK, Beel," muttered Lawali. "But before then I'll get the money. With Allah's help, I'll get it." He departed, sullenly.

There was to be a party at the German peanut oil factory outside of town. Visiting the factory from my mud-baked town was always a schizophrenic experience. In the middle of the African bush, springing up from the desert sand, was a miniature version of modern suburbia, complete with air-conditioned homes with sliding glass panel doors, flush toilets, running (and hot!) water, a swimming pool, and even a Ping-Pong

table. And yet it was a ghost town. Several years earlier a swarm of crick-
ets had destroyed the peanut crop, and the new, high-germinating seeds
brought in from Senegal turned out to be a bust. No peanuts, no peanut
oil. The factory had shut down completely, except for a confused, solitary,
and tippling German technician assigned to keep an eye on the unused
equipment and facilities. A group of burnt-out, desert-crossing German
tourists had stumbled upon the factory and their lonely compatriot.
Hence, the party.

Lawali had been over visiting when I left for the factory. For some
strange reason I decided to let Bobo, my faithful watchdog, accompany
me for the evening's festivities. So with Lawali outside the front gate, I
headed off for the peanut oil factory.

It was past midnight when I returned home. Although drunk on local
beer I sensed that something was askew. I checked my bedroom but
nothing was amiss: cheap watches, pens, pocket-knives, spare change. I
retraced my steps to the living room, and stared at the table. Gone! My
short-wave radio/cassette player had disappeared! It was then that I no-
ticed the glass pane missing from the side door.

Despite the late hour I ran through town to the Commissariat de Police. The gendarme on duty was even drunker than I. He directed me to
the Maison de Jeunes (Youth Center) where his superior was chaperoning
a student party. From the Maison de Jeunes the officer drove me home,
where he remarked that the opening from the glass was too small for any
human to squeeze through. It seemed even tight for the radio.

As I tossed and turned throughout the night, I could not help considering the rather suspicious circumstances surrounding the burglary.
The thief must have known I had left for the evening, for I usually spent
my evenings at home, retiring quite early. He must also have known my
watchdog was with me, for Bobo had a town-wide reputation for keen-
ness and ferocity. And, since nothing else was disturbed, the thief must
have known in advance what he wanted—the radio/cassette—and where
it lay. I drifted off uncomfortably, unsettled by suspicion. Could Lawali,
my own friend, have actually robbed me?

Mamane was aghast the next morning when I told him of the radio
theft. But he also took it in stride when I confided my suspicions. We
knew that Lawali was out carting at the time so we proceeded directly to
his home. I reminded his wife that Lawali had a goatskin of mine which
he had promised to tan months before. She led us to the room where

Lawali stored his meager possessions. We found my goatskin but not the radio.

Lawali acted rather oddly when we met for the first time following the break-in. Usually he greeted me informally. But this time, employing the Hausa body language of deference reserved for social superiors, he shook my hand formally, bowed his head, and did a little Hausa curtsy. He avoided my eyes, sighed uncomfortably, and offered to do chores. Even more strangely he never asked why Mamane and I had been to his home, an unusual visit that his neighbors would have commented on. Lawali was circumspect, discreet, and solicitous, not his usual insouciant, lively, inquisitive self.

Word of the theft spread rapidly through town, and sympathy was widespread. Heavily influenced by Sir Conan Doyle in my own youth, I deputized my students to keep an eye out for the radio: these were Niger's answer to Holmes's Baker Street boys. One of them suggested I see a marabout.

A marabout is an Islamic holy man, a Muslim priest. He memorizes the Koran, makes amulets, and establishes mysterious contact with the powers beyond. This particular marabout recommended that I have a chicken killed "so that the truth will come out. Someone will see the radio or have a revealing dream." Given the slowness of the police investigation to date, I wagered that a poultry sacrifice could be no less effective. So at my behest and expense, a chicken was slaughtered. (Only now do I wonder: what do they do with the body after the sacrifice?) But nobody saw the radio or recognized the thief in a dream. The marabout was forced to take the next, dire step: to cast a curse that would kill the thief if the radio were not returned within two days.

The day before the curse was to take effect I sent for Lawali. Although prayers were already said and the morning millet was already pounded—the sun had been up for at least an hour—Lawali was still asleep. This was strange, for if there is any generalization that one can safely make about Africans, it is that, barring illness, they do not sleep late. The reasons for Lawali's uncharacteristic slumber were disquieting. Mamane relayed that, according to Lawali's landlady, Lawali had traveled the day before to a village on the other side of the border, and returned not long before dawn. That was why he was still in bed.

Now, there is only one reason why Nigérien townspeople cross the boundary: business. Better stocked shops, more diversified markets, and an advantageous black market currency alone justify venturing into the perils of Nigeria.

Knowing that Lawali had engaged in nocturnal border-crossing clinched it for me. I was convinced that his scheme was to pay for my ox by hocking my radio.

I left word that Lawali should come to my house when he arose. He arrived a short time later, sensing trouble. He blanched when he saw my anger. Unable to contain myself, I grabbed him by the arm, dragged him into the house, and pointed at the radio-less table.

"Where is it, Lawali?" I demanded. There was no need to specify what "it" was, nor did Lawali pretend he had to ask.

"Allah, Beel, I don't know. I myself have tried . . ."

"The game is over," I interrupted in an uncommonly apt, literal translation into Hausa. "We're going to the police."

"Good!" he retorted, defiantly. Off we went, me smoldering, Lawali smiling, whistling, and singing.

When we reached the Commissariat, though, Lawali's "soul broke." The traditional *Salaam Aleikhum* stuck in his throat as we approached the gendarmes.

I explained the situation: Lawali's knowledge of my whereabouts at the time of the theft, his familiarity with my house, his changed demeanor. Admittedly, all such evidence was merely circumstantial; but for me, knowing Lawali as well as I did, it was conclusive. The police told me not to worry and that they would soon know the whole story.

Finally unburdening myself of mounting suspicion delivered an unfamiliar sense of relief. How liberating accusation can feel! When I returned to police headquarters that afternoon, however, I sensed that the investigation was not going well. The commandant himself wanted to see me, a sign that the proceedings had gone awry.

The commandant, a stuttering old bull of a cop, did not believe that Lawali was guilty. He had been trained in police work under the French and, faithfully adhering to the procedures and theories he had acquired through them, had failed to extract any information that would substantiate my version of the theft. We went over the events of the past five days, but the commandant was not satisfied. Lawali was called in.

Only then did I realize the enormity of having turned Lawali in. He was stripped to the waist, handcuffed, his usual insouciant smile gone. There were a few discrepancies in Lawali's version of his comings and goings of the last few days, but as far as the commandant was concerned they were minor. Lawali was led away.

"Y-y-you see, Monsieur Bill, since the night of the theft, there has been no ch-ch-change in the pattern of Lawali's visits to your home. Now nine t-t-times out of t-t-ten, the thief is not likely to return to the scene of the c-c-crime. It is extremely unlikely that, if Lawali was the thief, he would c-c-continue to frequent your p-p-premises." Stuttering made the commandant sound nervous, more the accused than the interrogator.

"M-m-moreover, you have known Lawali for well over a year. He has been a frequent g-g-guest in your house. In all that t-t-time, have you ever suspected him of stealing? No? And he has p-p-provided you with many f-f-favors in the use of his o-o-ox, hasn't he?"

It was now *my* reputation at stake. The commandant was implying that I had unjustly accused a friend, a poor oxcart driver, because I was upset over the loss of a mere electronic device. It was not enough that Lawali had betrayed and would soon be mocking me by his very release. Now I had to vindicate myself in the eyes of the commandant and the entire community. Otherwise, I would assume the reputation of an ungrateful, treacherous, peevish White Man. Proving Lawali's guilt had become a matter of my honor.

There were witnesses, I insisted to the commandant. Lawali told a boy who bumped into him outside my house the evening of the theft that he should not hang around "in case something gets stolen." Another man could confirm that Lawali had recently repaid a long-standing debt. And, of course, there was the woman who could confirm that Lawali had traversed the frontier not long after the theft of the radio.

Although still skeptical, the commandant was scrupulous. If only to show that he was taking my case seriously, he now decided to go through the motions of calling in witnesses and taking down testimony.

The first witness was Mamane, who related what he saw and heard the day following the theft. Two hours had passed since I showed up at the Commissariat de Police but it was only now that the commandant started to take notes. And what notes! The commandant scribbled furiously, interrogating in stuttered Hausa, transcribing into formal French, filling up sheaves of paper, writing in the margins, in the corners, turning the paper upside-down, sideways, every which way to write, record, transcribe. Just watching him was exhausting.

When Mamane left, the deputy commandant chimed in: "I think he did it, the houseboy."

This could turn ugly, I thought. Lawali exonerated, Mamane suspected, myself mocked. I thought of the slaughtered chicken and wished I had slaughtered two instead.

Enter Lawali's wife (with infant). The commandant starts with the routine questions, par for police school in France. But, as with much in former French West Africa, colonial methods are ill adapted to the rural African scene. Even Hercule Poirot, France's answer to Sherlock Holmes, would have been thrown for a loop.

"W-w-hat's-s your name?"

"Amadou."

"What's your last n-n-name?"

"Amadou."

"Amadou Amadou?"

"Who's that?"

"Is A-m-madou your f-f-first n-n-name?"

"No, Hadiza is."

"Who is Amadou?"

"My father."

(For my benefit: "Nom de famille, Amadou.")

"Where do you live?"

(Pointing to the east) "There."

"Your v-v-village's n-n-name?"

"Ingwalgamji."

"How old are you?"

Silence. Then, "I don't know."

"Apr-pr-proximately, please."

"Oh. I don't know. Maybe fifteen."

"Is this your only ch-ch-child?" And so on.

Close to three hours had elapsed and nothing conclusive had yet been established. My hopes were placed on the landlady, the woman who told Mamane that Lawali had been over the border. It was a significant claim that Lawali had consistently denied.

In she shuffled, an old frame of a woman, bent, wrinkled, cantankerous. The commandant, respectful of her age, was more subdued in his questioning.

With the preliminaries dispensed with, the commandant asked, "Have you said that Lawali went y-y-yesterday to the other side of the b-b-border?"

She seemed not to hear, and the commandant repeated the question in a somewhat louder voice.

"NO, NEVER!" she shouted in return.

I recoiled, certain all was now lost. My key witness turned out to be willing to lie to the police. If she lost her tenant to prison, she may have been reasoning, she would also lose her rental income. But there was no way I could challenge her. Things had gone sour enough, without my going head to head with an old African lady. The commandant thanked the woman and ordered an officer to escort her home. Mentally, I prepared for defeat and to take my leave.

But the commandant was not finished. Something, imperceptible to me, had clicked for him. For the second time he had Lawali called in.

Lawali entered, looking even more perturbed than in his previous appearance. He had a circle of sand on his forehead, the sign of the devout Muslim who touches his face to the ground in prayer. But the sand could not hide his agitation.

Lawali, sitting outside the commandant's chambers, had no idea what testimony had been proffered within. All he saw was a parade of summonees enter and depart, one by one: my housekeeper, his own wife, the old woman. Fear and curiosity wrestled together on his face.

"Lawali," began the commandant, "why didn't you tell us you had been to the other s-s-side?"

Silence. Flinching. Fear.

"Lawali," continued the commandant, "has anyone h-h-hit you today?"

Lawali forced open his lips to deliver a dry "No."

"Now I know, you hear st-st-stories, Lawali, of men being b-b-beaten. B-b-but that's only when we are f-f-forced to resort to such methods."

Silence.

The commandant opened his desk drawer. Slowly, he drew out an object that neither Lawali nor I had ever seen in our lives: a yellowing French language magazine for detectives. He opened the journal to a certain page and pointed to a photograph. It was a picture of a polygraph machine.

"Look at this, Lawali. Do you see this m-m-machine? Do you know that with this m-m-machine we can know if you are telling the t-t-truth or not? Yes, Lawali. You cannot hide the truth from us."

Nothing elevates the power of the written word like illiteracy. For the unlearned, that which is printed is magical, potent. Here in Hausaland, it was common practice to drink the dissolved ink from the wooden tablets on which passages of the Koran had been written. (This "medicine" tasted like turpentine.) But not only the holy written words of the Koran inspired awe: those of a crumbling magazine could be no less effective.

The fact that there was no lie detector within thousands of miles of our little town in no way diminished the commandant's ruse. The mere image of such a device was enough to terrify the conscience of my poor friend. Noticing the effect his photographic bluff had had, the commandant now softened his style. As if by a miracle, his stutter disappeared.

"Lawali, have we eaten anything this entire afternoon? Have we drunk anything?"

"No," came the murmur.

"Lawali, we're all hungry, thirsty, tired. We all want to go back to our families. But you won't permit us. We've been fair with you, Lawali, haven't we?" Lawali agreed.

"Ah, but I know why you haven't told us the truth. Because of shame. That's it. Shame. Now you"—he gestured to the other policemen in the room—"you get out of here! Now, that's better. "Sit down, Lawali. Go ahead, sit down. There's no one else here, just your friend Bill, me, and yourself.

"Lawali, I want you to do something for me. I want you to think of your wife. And your child, too. Is it worth all this, Lawali, this radio, to put them through such pain? Is the truth worth sacrificing for a mere machine?"

Lawali was visibly upset.

"Lawali, I want you to think of your friend Bill. You love Bill, don't you? Look, we all understand temptation—you go into his house, a White Man's house, a house of wealth and prosperity. It's understandable that you should desire those things which you see there. But we are your friends, Lawali, you can tell us. Well?"

Lawali turned and pierced me with his look. It was a look of apology, of regret, of yearning. He was about to explain, I felt sure of it, why he had betrayed me. Was it on account of Bange? Because I was leaving? For some other, hidden reason?

But the commandant was uninterested in mediating some interpersonal reconciliation. He wanted a confession of crime, not of broken trust.

"Lawali, how big is the radio?"

Lawali described it.

"Lawali, where is the radio now?"

In this sandy, Sahelian room, with the sounds of night (dusk having long since descended) the only reminder of the world outside, truth, guilt, and victory were about to emerge as one. It was the most poignant moment of my two years in Africa. Fate had rejected millions of other, more likely permutations for our respective lives, binding the three of us that evening in a West African police office.

And who were we? An impoverished peasant, a French-trained policeman and—me. And what was I? A hapless schoolteacher, who happened to have a lighter skin and foreign accent? An adventurer, an intruder? Or was I, in the searing words of Anton, my only black American friend back in college, merely "slumming" here in Niger?

"A fish vendor has it. On the other side of the border."

The moment had come and gone, and I was scarcely aware of it. Was this the taste of inquisitorial victory, I wondered, the perverse pleasure derived from outing the truth? It felt so hollow now. I wished we could all go home.

"How much did you sell it for, Lawali?"

Would this never cease? Is admission of guilt not sufficient for the professional truth-monger? Must he get to all of the embarrassing details immediately?

"I didn't sell it. I gave it to him, and promised to return next week. He'd give me the money then."

CRACK!

As if lightning had careened through the walls and struck him, Lawali was violently ejected from his seat and flung across the room. Stunned, crouched on the bare, cement floor, he now listened to the bellowing laughter of the commandant and his accomplice. This other policeman, on some secret signal by the commandant, had unobtrusively slipped back into the interrogation room and, standing behind Lawali, had without warning struck him from behind. I was as dazed as Lawali. Then he looked up at me, with an uncomprehending, wounded expression, and I thought: Who had betrayed whom?

The blow was for lying. The commandant refused to believe that Lawali had handed over my radio to the fishmonger without receiving payment. And he was right: Lawali now admitted that he really had been paid the equivalent of sixteen dollars.

CRACK!

This second blow from behind came because the commandant did not believe that Lawali had taken so little money for so valuable an object. But this part of the confession never changed and over the next several weeks elicited the same reaction from dozens of villagers:

"That Lawali. Not only does he steal from his *patron*, but he does it for mere pennies. An ingrate, but even more than that, a dope!"

Ensuing interrogations and further beatings rounded out the details. Lawali did not, as he had first confessed, enter through the window. Rather, he had surreptitiously pocketed a key to my side door when I was in my bedroom dressing for the peanut factory party. Later he unlocked the door, took the radio, and removed the window pane to make the theft look like a simple burglary. Of the sixteen dollars Lawali had garnered, five were used to repay an old debt and another five were spent on cassava flour and other foodstuffs. The remaining six dollars he gave to his wife.

Although the cross-border fencing of my radio technically violated international law, it would have been futile to seek redress through official legal channels. Even if the respective authorities of Niger and Nigeria were to take an interest in a petty theft suffered by a fleeting foreigner, I would have long since returned to America before the case was resolved. Instead, the commandant suggested that we tap the local network of traditional chiefs.

We concocted a plausible, semi-truthful story: a boy had borrowed his older brother's radio and sold it on a lark. Now the older brother wanted the radio back. Emissaries of "my" chief were sent to his royal counterpart on the other side of the border to explain our town's predicament. That chief contacted the fish vendor who agreed to sell back the radio at cost. Counting the requisite baksheesh, I repossessed my radio for the equivalent of twenty-five dollars.

To some people in my dusty, sub-Saharan town, the radio became a symbol of divine justice, of cosmic retribution. The improbability of its return, along with the perfidy of the thief, proved that Allah does not tolerate treachery. It is still in West Africa, my JVC short-wave radio/cassette player, venerated as a symbol of God's ultimate justice.

To the commandant, it was a successful—and potentially profitable—end to a difficult case. Would not the victim be grateful to him? The commandant conveyed to me his interest in buying Bange—at *un bon prix* (a good price), *bien sûr*.

One year after my teaching assignment ended, I was back in West Africa as a State Department intern and scheduled a short trip back to Magaria. Lawali had since been released from prison and, hearing that I was back, made a beeline back to Magaria from the small village where he was now living. He greeted me with his old, spontaneous joy, as if nothing untoward had ever transpired between us. There was no hint of resentment or embarrassment, not from Lawali. Bowled over by his exuberant welcome, I could not force myself to bring up the radio, our falling out, or his imprisonment. Long thereafter I regretted not having done so and wondered, wondered . . .

But three years later I did get a second chance. This time it was I who journeyed out to Ingwalgamji, Lawali's village, to come to grips with our past and tattered friendship. "Why did you do it, Lawali?" I forced myself to ask. "Why did you take the radio? On account of Bange?"

To my astonishment, Lawali expressed neither shame nor embarrassment for having stolen the radio. "It wasn't I who did it," Lawali explained, glad for the opportunity to finally square himself with me. "It was *bori*—spirit possession." He claimed that he had been bewitched into the theft—by whom, he could not reveal—and therefore was not in control of his actions. It was a simple case of temporary, involuntary possession of soul. His affection for me had never changed. Nor did Lawali blame me for turning him in: it was entirely reasonable.

It is to "do good," of course, that my government sends thousands of Peace Corps Volunteers to live and work in remote, impoverished corners of the globe. Perhaps I did make some worthwhile contribution during my own two years of high school teaching on the fringes of the Saharan desert. But none of my training could prepare me for the ache of loneliness that living in an alien culture inevitably entails. Nor did it warn me of the trap of compensating for such loneliness in relationships that are inherently skewed by unbridgeable differences in worldview rooted in insuperable gaps in material wealth.

For twenty years I processed Lawali's betrayal. Only afterwards did I begin to realize that, by so wanting to befriend him in the first place, it was I who had betrayed Lawali.

3

When the emotional toll taken by the Lawali betrayal began to wear off, I started to intellectualize the saga's lessons. One of them provided a pretext for returning to Hausaland: that traditional chieftaincies may operate more efficiently than modern bureaucracies, especially in international settings. What other aspects of local culture, I wondered, might that borderline illuminate? To what extent does belonging to Nigeria or Niger—those haphazard colonial creations—make a difference to the Hausa peasants who today find themselves on opposite sides of the boundary? Can modern notions of nationalism—Nigerian, Nigérien—compete with longer-standing ties of culture, language, and religion—those, say, of being Muslim, of being Hausa?

During my two years as a Peace Corps Volunteer in Magaria, I'd never once crossed the nearby border into Nigeria: too many visa hassles, too many scary stories about Nigeria. Now, a few years later, I was contemplating setting up scholarly shop in two villages on each side of the boundary. Negotiating the actual border crossings, I reasoned, could come later: no need to complicate the formal research proposal with the intricacies of West African immigration law. As a result, I wound up with three separate proposals: one for Niger, another for Nigeria, and yet another for the United States. Niger's Ministry of Higher Education and Scientific Research granted permission, and Uncle Sam funded me through the Nigeria Fulbright program.

Shortly before the deadline for activating the Fulbright, the Nigerian university denied my application. By schmoozing in Hausa at the Nigerian consulate in New York, though, I managed to secure the indispensable visa to Nigeria. Some weeks later, through the intercession of newly made friends in Nigeria—and despite the recommendations of a jealous senior colleague—I secured affiliation with another university.

With the help of an alhaji (a returned pilgrim from Mecca) in Kano, a marabout in Magaria, and a topographical site map (from the U.S. Army Corps of Engineers), I settled on Yardaje in Nigeria and Yekuwa in Niger as my sites of comparison. There was no road connecting the two villages. I would definitely need a horse.

A mile or so beyond the eastern outskirts of Yardaje, in the bleak, sandy brown landscape, incongruously towers a black, metal, ten-foot-high pole. Although the Hausa call it *tangaraho*—"telegraph pole"—no wires are attached and it signals no messages. Except for this symbolic one: at this spot Nigeria ends, and Niger begins.

Villagers traipse back and forth past the *tangaraho* as a matter of course. Technically, they are supposed to declare any commercial merchandise—including grains or livestock—that they transport across the border. Otherwise, says the law (recorded far away, in incomprehensible European languages), they are engaged in a criminal enterprise: smuggling. But to whom ought the poor villager make his declaration? Official border posts lie far away, to the east and to the west. For villagers it makes much more sense to risk the sporadically roving customs patrollers (usually from the Niger side of the border), who might confiscate the goods or extort baksheesh, than to follow a laborious, circuitous route that doubles the straight-shot eight-mile journey. So pitted against the "French" customs agents (for here Niger is still commonly referred to by the name of its erstwhile colonizer, *Faranshi*), reluctant borderline smugglers play a potentially costly game of cat-and-mouse. At least the rules are predictable.

But how would a mounted, border-crossing White Man fit into such a game? Whatever treaty or agreement, official or unofficial, that permitted Nigerian and Nigérien Hausa to walk across into each other's country surely did not cover an American on horseback. To do things by the book, each time I wanted to go from Yardaje to Yekuwa I would have had to travel to the Immigration Office and Aliens Police in Kano, well over a hundred miles away, to secure permission to leave the country and get a reentry permit stamped in my passport. This alone could take several days. If my multiple-entry visa for Niger had expired, I would also need to procure a new visa from the Nigérien consulate in Kano. Only then could I travel back to the border, crossing at the official immigration post at Babban Mutum where officials were usually doubly suspicious, and predatory, toward non-Hausa border crossers. Then there would be Nigérien immigration to clear at Tinkim—less corrupt but no less intimidating. Next stop, Magaria.

But in Magaria there is little public transport on the unpaved road to Tsatsumburum, off of which begins the footpath to Yekuwa, still several miles away. Now imagine reversing the entire journey, including travel

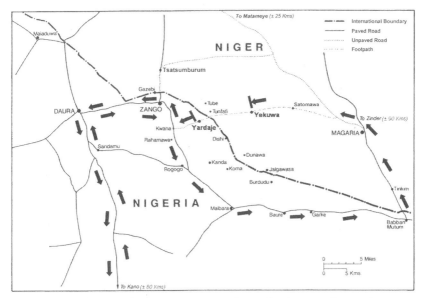

Yardaje and Yekuwa and environs. Arrows indicate the theoretical route for
documented road travel between the villages; practical alternative was to ride
a horse back and forth (eight miles each way).

to Kano to re-register with the Aliens Police, returning to Yardaje via
Daura and Zango. In short, for each visit between the neighboring villages I would have had to log at least five hundred miles and spend an entire week on administrative procedures and actual travel. (Had I initiated
such a journey from the Nigérien side of the boundary, I would have had
to add a thousand miles, and several more days, to obtain a visa from the
Nigerian embassy in Niamey, Niger's capital.)

Under the circumstances, I, like my village hosts, decided to take my
risks.

Still, I never crossed the *tangaraho* (at least not intentionally) without
holding a valid visa for the country I was entering. Yet it always seemed
irrelevant: whom would I encounter who would even know how to read a
passport? Once, however, I almost did get into big wahalla . . .

One lazy afternoon, roaming the bush after saddling up in Yardaje, I
suddenly found myself snout to mug with a stout soldier, all alone,
fiddling with his khaki pants and challenging me in frenetic French: the
Nigérien army! Each of us was quite startled: I because I thought I was

still in Nigeria; he because he hadn't expected to encounter a White Man in the bush, on *or* off a horse. The flustered soldier—he had just finished relieving himself when I appeared out of nowhere—ordered me to follow him to his commander. Still on horseback, debating if I should hightail it safely back deep into Nigerian territory, I sheepishly followed behind.

Nearby, in a sandswept encampment of Fulanis—simple herders who rarely gather in large numbers—a crowd of formally dressed nomads were engaged in formal proceedings. Overseeing the unusual affair was the *sous-préfet*, the commandant, of Magaria. Although no less surprised to see me than his bodyguard, the commandant was pleased to speak French publicly with the White Man who—miracle of miracles—happened to have his Niger research authorization on him. (Fortunately, it never came up that my little horse ride had originated in Yardaje—that is, Nigeria.) The *sous-préfet* invited me to join him in witnessing the investiture of a new chief for this band of Nigérien nomads, making sure that I took home some of the roasted guinea fowl that the Fulani had prepared in tribute.

"Vous avez la chance que je vous ai trouvé," the commandant told me at the end of the ceremony, with a patronizing air. "It's a good thing that I found you. In these parts, next to the boundary, if the peasants had come upon you like this, roaming around all by yourself, they would have tied you up and brought you to me in Magaria." I felt no need to disabuse the commandant of his exaggerated sense of Nigérien civic defense along the borderline. But I do wish I'd had the opportunity to inform him, or at least his overbearing aide-de-camp, what an onlooking Fulani told me shortly thereafter: that when the soldier first spotted me, I was, in fact, still in Nigeria; it was the *soldat* who had, in his search for a discreet spot to urinate, unwittingly drifted across the invisible boundary . . .

I suppose I was lucky, too, in the timing of my last horse ride across the boundary, returning to Yardaje, at the end of December 1983. At midnight on the following day military insurgents launched a successful coup d'état that put to death Nigeria's Second Republic. To prevent the flight of those politicians fearful of the soldiers' declared anti-corruption drive, Nigeria's Armed Forces Ruling Council officially closed the nation's land borders and instituted motorized patrols along its open frontiers. Fortunately, I had just bid adieu to Yekuwa and Niger: in a few weeks I would depart from the Kano international airport in Nigeria. When the Nigerian government decided the following March to change the nation's currency, it again officially closed the border—and kept it closed for two more years. Hapless border crossers caught by Nigerian patrols during that period were subject to humiliation: being made to run and "bark" like dogs; having to crawl like ducks; jumping on their hands, like frogs. Others suffered various kinds of torture: holding their ears, with arms under legs, for hours at a time; crawling on their knees and elbows, on pavement, until they bled; dragging their buttocks on a road strewn with rocks; being cut on the head with broken glass. Borderline normality returned on March 1, 1986, four months before my Fulbright was reactivated so that I could redo the lost surveys and update the boundary scene. Enter Sa'a.

Crossing the border on Sa'a was just like it had been on Wahalla, except that Sa'a was more of a scamperer. With a combination of trotting and cantering, we could cross from Yardaje to Yekuwa in an hour and a half. He was a gentle, obedient horse, not given to the wild outbreaks of his predecessor. Sa'a didn't even mind when my wife, who accompanied me for part of that visit, traversed the boundary with a cat on his back, the first phase of her transcontinental feline smuggling caper. (Loïza couldn't abide the idea that the furry white kitten we had adopted over the summer would likely have been eaten after our departure. Two years later, when we sublet Mousse-Mousse with our Boston apartment, the tiger-like creature with the startling eyes and strangely protruding ears went berserk on our subtenants and was committed to a local animal shelter.)

Toward the end of that rainy season, in the run-up to my departure, subtle (and not so subtle) suggestions were tendered from all corners. In Yardaje I was repeatedly asked, "Will you leave the horse with Mamane?" referring to my groom in Nigeria. "Will you leave it with Faralu?" they asked in Yekuwa, referring to my Nigérien horse keeper. The chief of Yekuwa said, "If you were moving to Niamey"—the distant capital of Niger—"then you'd leave the horse here. But where you are going is too far to do that." Implied was the small but enormously implicit tag ending *ko*: "Or is it?" All could see that Sa'a was a magnificent animal whom I'd fed quite well: millet and hay, every day. They thought it a shame to see such a horse disappear. So did I.

One day Faralu—my faithful, blunt, and indigent groom in Yekuwa—approached me about buying Sa'a. I was surprised. How could he possibly get enough money to do so? "I'll borrow it from different friends," he assured me. Was a horse previously owned by a Bature quite a status symbol?

"Would you keep it?" I asked, intrigued by the prospect of Faralu becoming the owner of the animal he'd been the groom for. "Would I find it when I next returned? Or would you sell it?"

"Oh, no! I would never sell it," Faralu responded, almost offended. "Only if I were to marry"—and for him, that meant taking a second wife—"or go to Mecca, only then would I sell it. But not for any other reason." Given the high incidence of both polygamy and pilgrimage in Faralu's family, these were not remote possibilities

Recalling how I'd sold Wahalla during my previous sojourn, Faralu asked if I'd want an advance.

"Yes," I replied cautiously, "but I'd need payment in CFA." Although Yekuwa belonged to Niger, an upstanding member of the French West African zone, its economy was so enmeshed in that of Nigeria that villagers trafficked only in internationally worthless naira.

My real concerns had little to do with currency convertibility, however. They were cultural, and spoke to my strange status as a fluent and functionally Hausa long-term village dweller unalterably wired to a Western psyche. Such contradictions bumped up against each other most severely in the African overlap between monetary and personal relations. They were aggravated by my also being, with respect to village costs and standards of living, an out-and-out tycoon.

Although I gave money to Faralu once a week, I did not employ him. He was my *yaro*, my boy, my protégé; I, his *mai-gida*, his protector, his patron. Faralu took care of my horse, traveled hither and yon at my behest, and performed multiple errands as they arose every day. But I did not *pay* him for any of this. What I gave him was not a salary: it was more of an allowance, but one which I always had to accompany with a little speech of thanks. By village standards it was, to be sure, a generous allowance; but in no sense was I obligated, in any formal sense, to give it to him. Had I skipped a week or two of allowances, perhaps even three or four, he would have had no basis to ask me for a red cent. He might have sulked, withdrawn, or disappeared: but the money was not his due, not in any contractual sense.

Here in Hausaland, where it is so scarce, money serves as a social lubricator. You spend what you need. If there is a surplus, you give it away. To whom? To those with whom you have established a certain relationship: to those who do for you, who praise you, who elevate you. The more you give, the grander you are. There is even a word for this relationship: *barantaka*.

My Western psyche says: my money is me. I part with it only when necessary, to purchase what I desire. When others expect me to give them money, just for themselves, I become suspicious, self-protective. I do not seek to give my money away to those with whom I regularly interact. My daily relationships with friends and co-workers ought to be based on intangible bonds of mutuality. Money destroys intimacy.

My Hausa persona, bowing to *barantaka*, says: give it away. Give the dirty cash to those who need it, whose life circumstances demand it. Do not hold on, as Westerners are selfishly wont to do, to those paper symbols of worth. Use the cold cash to cement some relationship. We are greater when we give our money away, not diminished. Cure yourself of the anality of retaining filthy lucre. Let it go!

To *sell* Sa'a to Faralu would have been not only the height of greed, but the closest approximation to exploitation as understood in Hausaland. By all rights, because I was his *mai-gida* I ought to have given Faralu the horse outright. But, even if I overcame my innate Western reluctance to confer large and expensive gifts upon non-family members, I couldn't give him my horse. For there was Mamane, Faralu's counterpart in Yardaje, to whom I was also bound by *barantaka*.

Selling Sa'a at all seemed less and less satisfactory. I imagined handing over the CFA francs—once converted from naira by a local market money changer—to some bored Frenchman in a foreign currency booth at Charles de Gaulle Airport. He would give me a stack of greenbacks in exchange. I would look at them, feel them in my hand, and think ruefully: "For this paper I have exchanged my beautiful horse? And what will I now do with this paper? How will I spend it? Frivolously, for sure. And rapidly—back home, these dollars will disappear fast. What will I buy that is worth a Sa'a?" I bristled at the folly of again exchanging my totem of freedom for a wad of sandy naira.

Most important, Sa'a could become a symbol: a token of trust and a promise of return. What greater act of faith than to leave my horse *saboda wata rana*—for some future time? Villagers far and wide would see my horse and be reminded of me. And I, even while ensconced in America, could retain Sa'a in my mind's eye and know that I still had a stake—a living, breathing, regal stake—in the hinterlands of Hausaland. And a material reason to return.

"How irrational!" my superego chided me. "You're going to keep a horse in Africa while teaching in America? For what? To satisfy an adolescent—or rather, childish—attachment to an adventure, a dream, a horse? Why can't you accept the fact that you—are—leaving? Why don't you just cash in the animal and forget it?"

"Because he's a wonderful creature," my Inner Child resisted. "Gentle, obedient, and beautiful. Sure, he eats like a horse—but he *is* one!"

"Good point," conceded Superego. "But who will take care of him?"

"The chief! The chief would personally see to it. He said so himself."

"Come on. Can you believe that? In this land of scarcity, of periodic famine? Even if you did manage to get back in a few years' time, you'd find some emaciated beast. Skin and bones. Who would take pains for someone else's animal—someone who is a world away?"

Inner Child pouted. "But he *promises*. And he's a *chief*. And everyone will know—this is Mista Bello's horse. *Kumya*—shame—will prevent him from being negligent. After all, if Sa'a is here, they'll ride him and want him to be in good shape. Without any other means of getting around, the chief has the best reasons in the world to ensure Sa'a would be well provided for.

"And he's a young horse," Inner Child remonstrated. "He'll grow bigger—and faster. He's got many years of spark left to him." And then Inner Child thought he could convince Superego with some adult language. "It's an investment, too. It's time to stop thinking small. A horse is something that will only increase in value. Especially in this inflationary economy. Think big, Superego. Invest!"

"You don't think a horse in Africa is somewhat of a remote investment? And how would you ever get your money out?"

"It's an international investment venture," Inner Child replied, weighing each of these big words seriously. "Look, if I later so instruct the horse-holders, even by letter, to sell it, they will. Someone will take the money to Magaria. Then they'll send it to me by international money order."

"You'll never see your horse again," Superego sighed. "Or your money. You're fooling yourself, letting yourself being talked into giving away an extremely valuable prize. How gullible you still are!" Superego didn't need to remind Inner Child about the ox deal gone awry in Magaria. He went on, "And what will the people of Yardaje say, you who have taken such pains not to show any favoritism toward either village?"

"Now it's you who are rationalizing," Inner Child replied. "I can do with my horse as I see fit. Anyway, I'll just explain, 'The chief of Yekuwa has offered to feed and take care of my horse until my return. How could I refuse such an offer?'"

The debate in my head intensified as market day approached. When the horse was not in sight, my Western, rational, professorial self carried the argument. But when I beheld, stroked and, especially, mounted Sa'a, it was Mista Bello who prevailed.

I was riding by an enormous locustbean tree in the bush when, for what must have been the hundredth time, a complete stranger called out to me, "You'll leave the horse when you go away, won't you?" All of a sudden I felt a surge of peace and happiness. For at that precise moment I said to myself, "Yes, indeed, I will leave my horse here. And he'll still be mine!"

Not long before my departure, I requested a Hausa pow-wow. Seated on mats in the open air courtyard were Danjuma the chief, Galadima (the "royal notary"), the chief's brother Alhaji Aminu, another elder or two, Faralu, and myself.

"I am soon to depart," I began. "But my heart is heavy, for I have become accustomed to you, and you have become accustomed to me."

"It is so," they murmured in assent.

"Beyond this, you have been accustomed to seeing me on my horse. It, too, is accustomed to living here."

"It is so."

"Now since Allah has seen fit to allow me to return here since I first went away, so I pray that He will enable me to return in the not too long future. If this comes to pass, then I pray that I will reunite once more with my friends in the village."

"May Allah protect us until that time."

"Amen," I responded, as is called for. "Now since I have grown accustomed to riding this one horse, it would also greatly please me to be able to ride it, too, whenever God brings me back."

"May it be Allah's will."

"And so," I continued, addressing Danjuma directly while careful, in deference to the chieftaincy, to avoid the overly familiar second-person pronoun, " I propose entrusting this horse, the one I call 'Luck'—to the chief. That way, he too can derive use and pleasure from it."

"It is good," the group assented.

"One would take care of it, as if it were a loan. If needed to journey to a baby naming ceremony, or to a marriage, or to a funeral—wherever one needed to go—the horse would be here. And the day that I return, it would be here for me as well."

"*Haka fa,*" came the group response. "Indeed."

The chief finally broke in to respond. "We have heard what you have said," he said, "and your idea is a good one. But there are things beyond man's control. There is disease. There is death."

"Yes, these things are indeed beyond us," I said, having anticipated an "acts of God" contingency. "Nobody can be held responsible for that which Allah has decided. If the horse becomes sick, or if it dies, then this is 'a matter of Allah.' There would be no blame."

"Then we agree to what you have proposed," Chief Danjuma declared. "Faralu," he said, gesturing toward my groom, "will continue to care for your horse. We will see to it that it be given hay, that it drink water, that it eat millet. And, if Allah wills, you will ride your horse when you return."

"May it be Allah's will," I concluded.

"Amen. Amen."

There was no question of drawing up a contract. To my mind it would be heavy-handed to insist, among illiterates, on a written document. Local norms dictated that oral agreement and witnessing were adequate. Was that not the case among the rural Hausa themselves? To now deviate from local custom and start imposing the way of the White Man—not to mention the legalisms of the American—would have signaled, would it not, a lack of trust?

But back in self-styled savvy Yardaje, where I was receiving an unexpected assemblage of predeparture well-wishers from around the region and over the boundary, there was consensus among my visitors that I had grossly erred. "You ought to have written it all down!" chided Gambo-the-Petrol-Seller from Zango, always quick to criticize my lack of savoir faire and to denounce the bumpkin ways of the bushmen. As for Souleymane, I ought to have left Sa'a with his provincial chief in Magaria, not with the village chief of Yekuwa. At their urging and dictation, I hand-drafted a document with copy (how quickly we've forgotten the convenience of carbon!) that my guests officialized by signing, leaving space for the signatures of Chief Danjuma and two other Yekuwa witnesses. It being market day, we easily found a visitor from Yekuwa who agreed to deliver the deed. A few days later, another "son of Yekuwa" trekked the eight miles back across the border from Yekuwa to Yardaje, returning to me the original document, now affixed with the signatures of the chief of Yekuwa, Galadima—the royal notary—and Faralu, my horse groom.

Yardaje, le 10 septembre, 1986

Yau, Laraba, ran goma da watan tara (septembre),
ni Mista Bello (watau William F.S. MILES), ina
niyyar bada ajiya doki akawal, wanda na
saya a Mai-aduwa naira dari shida, sunansa Sa'a, a
Mai-gari Alhaji Adamu Danjuma Yekuwa. Kotai. Hal lokacin
da na bukata, saydawa ko amsa ko badawa ga wanda na
bukata. Shaida Gambo Mai-Mai Zangon-Daura, da Sani
Dauda Yardaje da Mallam Suleiman Abba Magarya.

William F.S. Miles

MASU-SHAIDA YEKUWA

⎽   • Foralu

ƐN.   - Galadima

⏝   - Mai-bari

GAMBO
MAIMAI
ZANGO

Original horse deed.

4

Three years elapsed before I could return to Hausaland. But in the summer of 1989 the National Boundary Commission of the Presidency of Nigeria invited me to address a conference on the Niger-Nigeria borderlands. In attendance were the Emir of Daura in Nigeria and the Sultan of Zinder in Niger, two powerful chiefs with whom I had long-standing relationships . . .

As late as the 1970s one of the informal initiation rituals of a Peace Corps Volunteer in eastern Niger had been to pay honorific greetings to the venerable chief of Damagaram, a dusty but important town that the French had initially designated capital of their colony and preferred to call Zinder. He was a relic of the past, this sultan, a toothless old man in both the literal and political senses: literally toothless, because dental restoration is virtually unknown in traditional Africa; politically toothless, on account of unreversed colonial declawing after a previous sultan of Damagaram had murdered a couple of visiting French military officers. Surrounded by praise-yelling and sword-wielding bodyguards in bright red-and-green turbans and uniforms, the Sultan of Damagaram nevertheless was an impressive sight as he received PCVs, tourists, and other visitors in the spartan antechamber of his mud palace, his Royal Highness seated on an extraordinarily unimpressive mud throne. Speaking little French though having reigned throughout much of the colonial era, the sultan was stereotypically typecast for Foreign Legion movies set in French West Africa.

By the time my father Samuel visited me in the winter of 1978–79, the old sultan was dead and had recently been replaced by one of his sons. The new sultan was himself firmly anchored in the "modern" Niger: not only could he speak French but he could drive (indeed, he had been the late chief's chauffeur) and was generally enamored of all kinds of gadgetry, vehicular and otherwise: so many phones were installed in his palace receiving room that his Highness was prone to answering the wrong one. My father and the sultan hit it off famously, he gifting Dad with a royal dagger and my father reciprocating by mailing the sultan a pair of designer sunglasses from New York City. Elderly White Men being virtually unknown in this part of Africa, my white-haired father was as much a sensation in the sultan's palace as he was in my Peace Corps post. Nearly a quarter of a century later, Dad's visit is still recalled in Magaria; in 1989, the sultan expressed genuine sympathy for my father's passing seven years prior.

The Emir of Daura, on the other hand, had already achieved a high measure of notoriety and achievement in Nigeria when I first introduced myself in 1983. A one-time government minister who had himself reigned during the British era, the emir subjected me at our very first meeting to a tougher examination than had any of my professors during my Ph.D. orals a few months prior, testing me on the spot, in front of his royal court, on the history of his emirate. I must have passed, for he blessed my stay in his territory.

Assembled in the conference hall with the Emir of Daura and the Sultan of Zinder were a host of other high-ranking chiefs whose kingdoms touched the Niger-Nigerian border, military officers governing the border states, academics working on boundary issues, and assorted officials performing duties of protocol. One of them secured for me a visa for Niger—the Sultan of Zinder promising me a ride home in his convoy—and reentry permit for Nigeria, allowing me to visit Yekuwa and return to Nigeria through normal, legal channels. (As it turned out, when I traveled with the sultan no one checked—much less stamped—my passport at either border post.) For his part the Emir of Daura publicly bestowed upon me an additional nickname: "Son of Daura."

It was heady to think how my work in backwater villages had now put me among this élite set of border managers—so heady that I dared to confound the interpreters (just as Ali Mazrui, the eminent scholar, had when addressing the Organization of African Unity in Swahili) by addressing the plenary session first in English, then in French, and then in Hausa. So keen was I to establish my linguistic credentials that I publicly committed a politically counterproductive and culturally serious faux pas.

After presenting the results of surveys that I had conducted in both Yardaje and Yekuwa—surveys that pointed to a higher level of national than ethnic consciousness—I related, in Hausa, a recurrent dream that I'd had. It was a nightmare, really: a barbed-wire fence had been erected along the border, physically separating neighboring villages. (Although I didn't divulge these details, in my dream Yardaje had been built up into a veritable town, with multiple-storied buildings, paved roads, traffic, and—contrary to Islamic law—an alcohol-serving beverage bar. The folk of Yardaje were now jaded, indifferent to the visit of outsiders and preoccupied with drinking booze, playing cards, and making money.)

I concluded my narration expressing the fervent wish that my dream not become a reality and that the border never become a force for separation. But my cautionary moral was for naught, the gaffe complete; for in Africa remembered dreams are regarded not as windows into the past, but prophecies upon the future. Rather than cautioning lest the Niger-Nigeria border become a barrier between the Hausa living on each side, I had stupidly forecast that very outcome.

Even after diplo-academic honorifics, a broadcast of me speaking Hausa on Nigerian television, and a chauffeured ride in a sultanic caravan, it was sheer joy to return to the unpretentiousness of the African bush and reunite with friends and horse alike. Sa'a was a little skinnier than I had remembered him but no less spunky. As Faralu saddled him and I mounted, Inner Child—in restive incubation during the intervening years of tenure trackdom—reemerged triumphantly, beaming with vindication. "You see," he whisperingly boasted, "I told you. Here you are, back in Hausaland, on *your* horse, and you can ride, ride, ride . . ."

Ride I did, galloping and whooping loudly, cowboy-style, as we kicked sand—just as before. Father that I was now—my daughter Arielle having been born two years earlier—I soon easily succumbed to the entreaties of the village's little children to allow them a ride, reestablishing one of my nicknames: Mallam Beel na Yara, "the One Who is Close to Children." Out in the bush on the outskirts of the village one brilliant morning, one after another I plucked the children up onto Sa'a with me, cradling them around the stomach for security as we trotted in circles under an enormous baobab tree. It felt like giving pony rides in a village fair, but with the bittersweet knowledge that it would be a once-in-a-childhood treat. Given the paucity of village horses and the limitations on Hausa children's play, for most of the boys this was their only opportunity to get on a horse. And as for the girls, given the added strictures on female comportment among the Muslim Hausa, it was certainly the only time in their lives that they would be allowed to ride on any kind of animal at all. For even in Yekuwa, the prenuptial practice of bringing the virgin girl on horseback to her groom's house has now been abandoned. *Lokacinshi ya wuci*, I was told. "Its time has passed."

Traveling to Niger in the royal convoy after the conference adjourned reversed the expected order of my arrival in the villages: instead of arriving with fanfare by car in Yardaje on the main road on the day I had previously communicated, I quietly entered the village several days later from behind, riding in on Sa'a from Yekuwa. *Akwai wayo*, the Yardaje men teased me thereafter. "You really are a sly one: tricking us into waiting for you in front of the village on one day, and then sneaking into the village from the rear side the day after. "*Akwai wayo*, Mallam Beel. You're quite a trickster."

Since I had first arrived in Niger with the Peace Corps in 1977 until the borderlands conference in 1989, no more than three years had elapsed between successive visits to Hausaland. But after that, although I did manage to maintain this schedule for subsequent returns to West Africa—southern Nigeria in 1992, Chad in 1994, Burkina Faso in 1997—a whole decade slipped by between my last mounted traversal of the Nigerian-Nigérien frontier and receipt of the father-son trip-triggering letter from Yekuwa. Deciphering priestly handwritten *boko*—florid Hausa dressed up in Roman characters—no longer came easily.

For sure, in the interim I had run into Hausa-speakers in some of the most unlikely places on earth. In 1991, on the South Pacific island of Efaté, I'd stunned a black United Nations technical adviser when, correctly intuiting from his name and previous UN posting, I nonchalantly switched into Hausa during our interview. (His Oceanic workers burst into laughter when they saw their boss's dumbfounded reaction. He himself was a Ghanaian, but his mother hailed from northern Nigeria.) Three years later, while exploring the narrow byways of the Old City of Jerusalem, I amazed both my Nigerian Igbo colleague from Hebrew University and Alhaji Jedda, the local *mukhtar* (or neighborhood chief) of the Muslim African quarter, when we discovered that the only common language between Jedda and us was—naturally—Hausa! (The Chadian-born Jedda had grown up in northern Nigeria half a century before and never returned to Africa after his pilgrimage to Mecca. So it was to me he turned for news of the old country . . .) It was not so unusual to discover Hausa-speaking neighborhoods and their chiefs in N'djamena and Ouagadougou, the capitals of Chad and Burkina Faso; I was surprised, though, to discover that in "Ouaga" there were *two* Hausa chiefs—one for the Hausa whose families hailed from Nigeria, the other for those who had come from Niger.

But each of these countercultural encounters demonstrated the deterioration of my Hausa. With my Ghanaian interlocutor on Efaté, my Hausa speech was often blocked by Bislama, the Pidgin tongue of the

South Pacific; in Jerusalem, it was strewn with Hebrewisms. Letters from Lawal Nuhu, my schoolteacher friend who lived in Yardaje, gradually anglicized, perhaps in tacit recognition of my failing Hausa. It was from one of Lawal's letters, in fact, that I was apprised of an early horse complication: within a year or two of my last visit to Yekuwa in 1989, Sa'a had been traded in for a horse of another color—royal white.

Naturally, the indirect way in which I learned of my horse's disposal irritated me. Why had I not been notified—much less sought out for horse replacement authorization—directly from the concerned parties in Yekuwa? But for several reasons I decided not to pursue the matter then.

For one thing, I could easily intuit the motives for the horse switch. Although I often refer to Yekuwa as a single community, I mentioned before that it is in fact two distinct villages that over the years have expanded so as to bump up right against each other. (Once upon a time, there was only one Yekuwa; and then there was a mysterious scission, which may have been related to a false accusation of murder . . .) Each of the Yekuwas has its own chief: the chief of Yekuwa-Hamada, where I did not live, rode a stately white stallion when I lived in Yekuwa-Kofai. Sa'a, whom I'd left with the chief of Yekuwa-Kofai, was not of a chiefly color. The chief of Yekuwa-Kofai needed a white horse. Simple.

Furthermore, I didn't wish to inflict *kumya*—shame—from afar. Should my first correspondence in years relate to a disturbing rumor I'd heard—from across the border in Nigeria, no less—about an alleged breach in my "sign of trust"? Better to wait until my next actual return to Hausaland, and receive the explanation (or apology) in person.

Finally, I reasoned, after all these years, what did the color of my African horse matter? "It" was still my horse. Wasn't it? That "it" was no longer Sa'a did, admittedly, bother me a bit. More critical, though, was my continued claim to *a* horse in Yekuwa. As the years passed, *any* equine would do, as long as I could still tell my children that there was a horse awaiting them in Africa.

Thus had my horse problem evolved by the time I sat down to read The Letter from Yekuwa.

Anthropology has long dismissed the myth of the neutral participant-observer. In hindsight one wonders what could have been more naïve than the notion that a person from a strange and rich part of the world—usually of a higher status and another color, speaking the local language imperfectly (if at all), and arriving with unknown gadgets and

29-12-98

Wasika daga hannun El-hadji Malan
Harouna Zuwa ga Mista Bello. Gaisuwa mai
yawa da fatan alferi. Bayan haka muna
fata kana lafiya tare da iyglanka.

Ina bakin cikin Sanar da kai
cewa Allah ya ji wa Maigari Danjuma
Adamu rasuwa. Ya rasu ranal Laraba
7-10-98. Allah Jikansa.

Akwai sudani game da dokinka, masu
gado sun ce dokin nasu ne za su
sanya shi cikin kayan gado, Saboda
haka ka aiko da amsa cikin gaugawa
domin ka warware wannan rudani.
Idan akwai sheda a rubuce wadda kuka
Ji da Marigaji Danjuma a bisa Malla kar
dokin naka to ka hado da cikin
amsarka cikin gaugawa. Duk jama'a
lafiya suna gaida ka. Ka huta lafiya
Sai naga amsa.
                    Nine
          El-hadji Malan Harouna Rabiu
                Jekoua

Letter announcing the death of the chief and the inheritance dispute.

creature comforts—could blend into an alien community without untowardly disturbing it. But such was the positivism of the early discipline.

Even those fieldworkers most dismissive of researcher objectivity nevertheless felt compelled not to unduly muck up the community they'd come to study. You do not wish to supplant the local ruler and assume a leading role in a real-life "The King and I." Nor do you wish to become the spur for contention or warfare. Your goal is to blend in as nondisruptively as possible and to *record* the community's unfolding history, not to *make* it. You note, you leave, you write, you publish. Your overseas exploits launch your career. And then? Until the poststructural turn of the 1990s, such questions were not at the forefront of ethnography. Since then, happily, questions of conscience and responsibility have increasingly pervaded the hearts and printed pages of professional cross-culturalists.

If you are bound to maintain the relationship, *how* do you do so, in the absence of literacy and telephones? While much ink has been spilled on the (im)possibility of fieldwork neutrality, the ethics of (dis)engagement have only within the last decade or so become a major preoccupation of Westerners from a variety of disciplines and backgrounds, including historians, political scientists, and Peace Corps Volunteers.

Still, when it comes to any individual case, such notions as the "ethics of ethnography" are themselves problematic. Is it not paternalistic to relegate a relationship to the realms of exoticism and scholasticism, merely because African villagers are concerned? Was my horse dilemma academically curious, comically bizarre, or tragically serious?

American friends to whom I confided my African horse problem were at a loss: why, after all these years, did I still care about my rights to an animal in far-off Africa? Was it worth a lot of money? Why didn't I just forget the whole matter?

Because, I tried to explain, to neglect the horse affair would be a dismissive, patronizing kind of betrayal. It would also be a kind of suicide: the death of Mista Bello, my Hausa persona in the village of Yekuwa.

On account of the legalistically religious aspects of the dilemma, I approached two local authorities for canonical advice: a Muslim scholar and my rabbi. Neither could provide the clear-cut guidance I sought.

"How would shariah deal with such a property and inheritance dispute?" I asked Dr. Shawkat Toorawa, a Muslim from Mauritius. Although I knew that in the village itself African custom might trump Koranic law, it would still be helpful to know beforehand how Islamic jurists would adjudge the rightful heir question.

"Well," answered my young but full-bearded friend, "it would depend on which school of shariah they follow there. Is it Maliki? Hanafi? . . ." I was stumped. All previous attempts to determine denominational affiliation level had met with the same village response: *Musulmi kawai* ("We're just plain old Muslims"). I never figured out if the answer signaled a front of religious unity or an indifference to highfalutin' theological distinctions.

Rabbi Wayne Franklin of Providence did not ask if my Muslim African acquaintances inclined toward the Babylonian or Palestinian Talmud, the equivalent of the Maliki-Hanafi divide. Neither of us actually presumed that *halacha*—Jewish law—carried any weight in Hausaland. But disputed ownership of a dead chief's twice-removed horse would be precisely up the ecumenical alley of any expert whose legalistic training begins with a case of ox-goring. Or so I thought.

As I explained the detailed reasons for my son's and my imminent African journey, seeking some Semitic precedent of possible relevance, Rabbi Franklin took an unexpected tack. Rather than providing a detached talmudic perspective based on rabbinic reason, this modern, clean-shaven, ever-poised cleric of a Conservative Temple turned kabbalistic on me.

"You've left part of your *neshuma* there," he pronounced.

Even before my likening of the Hausa village to a pre-Holocaust *shtetl*, a community in which everyone is connected and a place to which you viscerally belonged, my rabbi understood. He saw that there still was a part of my *neshuma*, my soul, wandering horseback south of the Sahara. Did this *neshuma*, now sobered by fatherhood, still require an actual horse to claim as its own in Africa?

It is not that I wore my Jewish identity on my sleeve. But it was not my inclination to hide it among those who mattered to me in America, and I would not do so in Hausaland. Religion is in any event too important a topic *not* to discuss with Nigériens, and my interlocutors were invariably intrigued to learn how Allah is worshiped by others. Dan Mallam, a marabout whom I had befriended in Yekuwa in 1983–84, was particularly delighted.

Dan Mallam was one of the most wiry and physically expressive persons I have ever known anywhere. His facial expressions were as animated as his bodily ones. His every sentence pulsed with excitement. He was also one of those otherwise anonymous millions known in academic textbooks and development reports as "the poorest of the poor."

Dan Mallam and one of his friends were seated outdoors on his one piece of furniture—a straw mat. We were chatting in Hausa about nothing in particular when Dan Mallam asked me, in a completely matter-of-fact tone, if Isa was going to return. Isa is Arabic for Jesus.

"How am I supposed to know?" I shrugged.

"Oh, you know all right," he retorted in mock pique. "You just won't tell!" Yet there seemed also to have been a streak of genuine peeve, as if I was deliberately holding back from my hosts some critical information: *when* this shared Christian-Muslim prophet was scheduled to make his reappearance. It was the moment to reveal to Dan Mallam that I was not, as he had been assuming, a(n A)Nasara—a follower of "the one from Nazareth"—but rather a Bayahuda.

"Oho," responded the imam, "you don't follow the Prophet Isa. You follow the Prophet Musa." To the now thoroughly confused friend, Dan Mallam explained the difference among White folk between the followers of Isa and the Yahudawa, "they who follow the *atora* (Torah)." Then he turned to me to confirm something. "You were under the Faruna, weren't you?"

Faruna, faruna. What was Dan Mallam talking about?

"You don't know the Faruna? Harsh masters, they made your people work hard, so finally you left them." Aha! Faruna was their way of saying Pharaoh. When I confirmed the Faruna reference, Dan Mallam turned back to his friend, pointed at me as an illustration, and recounted how my brothers fled Masar (Egypt), were pursued by the Faruna, and had the Red Sea split for us. The friend sat bolt upright.

"That was you?!" he exclaimed in utter amazement and admiration. "You are the ones who did all that?"

I shyly admitted that it was indeed "us."

With clenched fist, he raised his arm and shook it at me, in the traditional Hausa salute extended to kings and rulers. He then uttered the words of praise reserved for such occasions (*Ranke ya da'de*—May you live long!) and exuberantly continued to recite the story of the Exodus, complete with miracles, with an immediacy, enthusiasm, and faithfulness beyond any I had experienced in the more than twenty Passover seders that I could recall. Moses' rod seemed to be his favorite feature. "Your brothers did all that? *Ranka ya da'de!*"

"Well," I explained with false modesty, "we had to. After all, we were living under a harsh regime." I used the local term for the colonial period under the French. "We also"—as was the case in Hausaland—"experienced slavery."

"Do you have the *atora* here with you?" Dan Mallam asked me, expectantly.

"No," interrupted the friend. "He has it at home. How could he bring it here? One needs a camel to carry the Torah."

I didn't bother to correct him. But in every subsequent Simchat Torah, the festival in which all the scrolls are removed from the ark and danced with, in my mind's eye I see a Torah-laden dromedary parading around the synagogue sanctuary.

The decade and a half following my revelation with Dan Mallam saw the spread of fundamentalist Islam in northern Nigeria and in Niger. But I refused to allow whatever fanaticism had taken hold outside of "my" villages to color my relationships within them. To do so would have meant ceding the essential humanity of person-to-person bonding to primal fear and regressive tribalism.

This is no idealistic, let's-all-hold-hands-and-sing-kumbaya sense of humanity. If I was going back to Yekuwa now, it was to protect my own property claims against local interlopers, even if I had to fight to do so. This is also a universal feature of the human condition. And I wouldn't renounce my horse rights in this Muslim land just *because* I was Jewish, and even if amputation for thievery and stoning for adultery were being reinstated as the law of the land in northern Nigeria. I am who I am, and this horse was mine—and my son's.

Years later, Rabbi Franklin would pay to have a water well dug for the pupils of the Yekuwa middle school. That would trigger a whole other set of disputes, as it turned out—but that's another story altogether.*

While wholly impractical, even in America owning a horse in Africa does command some social capital: think of Sa'a as a status symbol. There are Americans who impress by tooling around in Porsches and BMWs; by sailing in yachts; by owning cottages on the Cape. These status symbolizers need not even actually show off their boasted car, ship, or house. Mere mention of the expensive toy arouses desired envy.

And so it has been with us: we too gain status through the simple assertion that, regardless of our actual financial condition, we lay claim to a horse cared for by an African chief. Like a seldom handled heirloom in the family vault, just knowing it is there—and being able to remind the children every so often—provides sufficient psychosocial uplift.

* "The Rabbi's Well: A Case Study in the Micropolitics of Foreign Aid in Muslim West Africa," *African Studies Review* 51:1 (2008): 41–57.

5

For a long time, I had known that I was going to Africa with my dad—going to Africa on an adventure and on a mission. I felt very excited, nervous, and privileged. That I was going to Africa because of the horse was pretty interesting in itself—traveling halfway around the world just so I could see and ride my horse! I felt like some millionaire who had just bought a whole nursery day care center for my two week old baby. It gave me the feeling that I could do anything I wanted, anywhere, anytime. That's a handful of feelings!

What trust a boy puts in his father! As long as I'd be with him, Sam would willingly go anywhere: to Africa, to Hausaland, to Mars. Danger, discomfort, disgust—none of this would count, as long as we were together.

Two contradictory imperatives incessantly tug at me throughout our trip: adventure and protection. This is to be no tourist safari to Kenya, where during the day Bwana-bored guides point out lions from within air-conditioned vehicles and at night big-game photographers repose in four-star bungalows. In bringing Sam to the exotic but impoverished West African bush I am initiating him into a world simultaneously repugnant and alluring. On the one hand I am deliberately planning to expose my ten-year-old son to the economic ends of the earth, where tropical disease is common, infant mortality runs rampant, and local food and water pose constant gastric threats. It is also, on the other hand, an exotic and welcoming land where I have cultivated long-standing ties, entered into complex relationships, and developed deep feelings.

The day before we left I was very nervous. I couldn't remember a trip when the whole family wasn't going together—no sister, no mother. I also felt it would be cool to go to Africa—like camping for ten nights!

What does a father wish to give his child, if not the best part of his own life? While I do everything in my power to protect my son from direct harm, I shall not shelter him from the most intense land of my life—Hausaland. I shall share with him the dignity of life in impoverished Africa.

So I warn Sam about the flies. About the open-air latrines. About being stared at, about being touched. I tell him about the disagreeable smells,

The bearer of this notice, _____William Miles_____ served as a

Peace Corps Volunteer for __24__ months in Niger where the following

indicated diseases were prevalent .

Amebiases	Relapsing fever
Brucellosis	Yaws
C'olera	Intestinal Nematodes
Dengue Fever	Hookworms
Filariasis	Ascariasis
Onchocerca Volvulus	Intestinal Cestodes
Trichinosis	Taeniasis
Leprosy	Other Flatworms & Tapeworms
Yellow Fever	Leishmaniasis
Malaria	Cutaneous
Mucocutaneous	Plague
Schistosomiasis	Typhus
Tropical Ulcer	Trypanosomaisis
Hepatitis	

Date : 2 July 1979   J. Sonnemann, MD
                            Peace Corps Physician

Reasons not to take a ten-year-old.

about body odors from kids who haven't the access to water for washing. I make sure he knows in advance that not all people—especially nursing mothers and uncircumcised boys—are fully clothed. I don't wish to omit anything about which he can later cry, "But Dad, you didn't tell me about *this!*"

Still, there are the unpredictables. That is the nature of Africa.

I eagerly anticipated what I'd wish I'd brought, so I ended up packing a lot of entertainment—crayons, books, electronic games. Clothes I left for mom and dad to pack.

The first unpredictable occurs—predictably—before I would ever have predicted it: prior to takeoff in Amsterdam. Three rows behind us, on the mostly white passenger plane, a stout black man is shrieking. "Look at what you have done!" he wails accusingly at the three burly white men hovering around him. "You have broken my hands!" Tears stream from his eyes. "Oh, Aje," he weeps, invoking the name of an African deity. "Aje, see what they have done! My hands are broken. Broken!"

"Dad, what's the matter with that man?"

It isn't difficult to figure out. A quick glance reveals that the bemoaned hands are in handcuffs and that the shrieker's "companions" are, albeit in civilian garb, policemen. Here, as we are still sitting on the runway, Sam's first journey to West Africa is marred by this shocking scene.

A petite Dutch stewardess hurries over to reassure us. "Don't worry about that man," she says, with a broad but forced smiled. "He thinks that by making a big fuss now he can still leave the plane. That's how he was on the previous flight. He'll calm down once we're in the air and he realizes that it's too late and there's no getting out of it."

"It" means deportation. Whence he is being evicted, and for what reason, remains a mystery. Nevertheless, I have to supply maximum details, and my own variety of reassurance, to my apprehensive and curious son.

The stewardess is right, however. Once aloft the deportee does pipe down and, along with his fellow passengers, quietly watches the in-flight movie.

Four hours later, having crossed the Mediterranean Sea and Sahara Desert, the pilot deadpans a personally alarming message. "Ladies and gentlemen, this is your Captain speaking. Because of the lack of visibility caused by the Harmattan dust clouds, we may not be able to land in Kano. It's quite common for this to happen during this time of year. If necessary, we'll fly over to Accra and try again from the coast later this evening. We'll keep you informed when we hear from Ground Control."

Immediately I think of Jeff and worry: is Sam thinking the same thing?

Six weeks earlier Jeff Metzel, a very close friend from school and a development consultant for Africa—son of Southern Baptist missionary parents and the father of two young children—had also boarded a plane for Nigeria. It too was forced to overshoot its destination on account of the Harmattan and land at a coastal airport. Shortly after taking off again, later that night, for a landing in Nigeria, Jeff's airplane crashed in the murky waters off the Ivory Coast. There were few survivors. Jeff was not one of them.

As chance would have it, Sam had been alone at home when the telephone rang from Africa, conveying the news of Jeff's demise:

"Sam, this is Andy Cook. I'm calling from Mali. May I speak with your father or your mother?"

"Hi, Andy! No, they're not home right now."

Pause.

"Sam, I'm afraid I have some sad news. There was an airplane crash in Africa. Jeff Metzel has died. You'll need to tell your parents."

A few minutes later my wife returned to the house to find Sam sobbing uncontrollably. Only a month before our two families had together ushered in the new millennium at First Night festivities in Boston. Like me, Jeff had a son and a daughter. Our sons shared the same age and first name.

As our own plans for traveling to Nigeria and Niger advanced, Sam had naturally been concerned about our own air safety. A proud ten-year-old does not convey his fears directly, though. "What airplane company was Jeff using?" Sam asked, nervously.

"Kenyan Airlines."

"Dad, what company are we going to travel with?"

"KLM."

"Is KLM a good airplane company?"

"The best!" I reassured him. "It stands for Royal Dutch Airlines." Stressing the royalty, I hoped, would impress his fable-reading self.

"Whoof," he exhaled, seemingly relieved.

Now, flying twenty thousand feet above the Sahel, my son turns to me and asks, "Dad, how come we can't land in Nigeria?"

How do you comfort your child when you yourself are trapped, power-less, and stricken with impending doom?

Ground Control does clear us and we land, with nary a bump, at Aminu Kano International Airport. I am so relieved that I forget a number of items on board, including a hand-made pair of leather, custom-fitted san-dals and their case with which my wife had gifted me twelve years before when we were living in southern India. "Forget about the sandals," she is probably telepathizing. "Just bring me back my son!"

Whatever rush of adrenaline you get from arriving in a foreign air-port for the first time, ratchet it up geometrically each time you fly into Nigeria. What indignity, what probing, what shakedown will you be subject to this time? Will having a ten-year-old boy in tow make you ex-empt or all the more vulnerable?

The very first time I flew into Lagos I was initially refused entry at im-migration for lack of a return air ticket. That I had documentation prov-ing that I was stationed with the Peace Corps in neighboring Niger, to which I could easily return overland, made no difference to the immigra-tion agent. He had espied an irregularity and already had dollars in his eyes. I was twenty-two years old, a traveler on a shoestring budget, and a virgin briber.

"May I explain my situation to a supervisor?" I naïvely queried.

The agent guffawed. "You want to talk to *him*?" He gestured with his thumb to his sidekick, with whom the windfall would presumably be split. Michael Feldman, my traveling companion, had already been admit-ted into the country. He was out of sight. My mental torturer was now gesturing to the plane from which we'd just disembarked, saying I would have to get back on. "To where?" I asked.

"I don't know. Ethiopia, maybe. It is not my problem."

Six words were all it took to initiate serious negotiations. Why were they so hard for me to utter? Perhaps because I knew that by saying them, I would finally enter that gray zone that—as much out of stinginess as principle—I'd successfully eschewed so far. Now, though, there was no way out.

"Isn't there something I can do?"

The agent hesitated not a nanosecond. He scribbled an astronomical sum on a piece of paper and waved it at me.

"But I don't have any dollars," I pleaded, in literal truth. "Only travelers checks." I reasoned that uniformed extortionists dislike financial complications. I was wrong. Immigration Agent merely suggested that I cash the checks at the airport currency exchange booth. "What about CFA?" I counteroffered, referring to French West African francs. "That I have in cash." Immigration Agent made some calculations and wrote down a figure in CFA that was twice the equivalent of the suggested dollar payment.

When the bargaining was done and we had settled on a mutually agreed upon figure—the equivalent of twenty-five dollars—Immigration Agent bestowed three weeks longer on my entry visa than I'd requested— "in case you like it and want to stay more"— and smilingly wished me a pleasant stay in Nigeria.

For sure, that was Lagos, capital of African graft. Kano airport could never compete with Lagos for the potential to traumatize. But even there, "irregularities" could prove costly.

Five years after the shakedown at the Lagos airport, I flew into the dusty airport in Kano to commence my Fulbright research scholarship. All papers, tickets, visas, etc. were in impeccable shape. Only the most creative government-employed extortionist could invent a pretext for a shakedown.

"Aha! Your yellow fever vaccination card is not in order. We will have to inject you."

A bluff, I snickered inwardly. All my initial vaccinations—cholera, smallpox, hepatitis, typhoid, meningitis, rabies—had been duly administered and recorded by the Peace Corps doctor in 1977. Yellow fever inoculations are valid for ten years; this was only 1983. I had shown the yellow World Health Organization card at various airports numerous times, and never had there been a problem.

"We do not know when it was given. It is not valid. You need to be revaccinated."

Now I examined my well-worn card as if for the first time, with the eyes of a professional proofreader. Incredible! Whereas the rubber stamp markings for all the other inoculations clearly indicated 1977, on the yellow fever sheet the fourth digit had never inked through. Never mind the identical date and signature for all the other recorded shots: this one was defective.

"What can be done?" I asked, slipping into defeatist mode.

"We will need to inject you."

"Where?"

"Right here. At our airport dispensary."

Although I still believed the Health Officer was bluffing, skeptical that such a ramshackle port of entry even kept yellow fever vaccines in stock, the vivid image of being stuck in the arm with a dull, well-worn needle in a dark corner of this African airport did have a sobering effect on me. How much would *you* bribe to avoid such a fate?

Behind the gate at the immigration counter a number of men in flowing robes and brimless conical hats await Sam and me. There is Lawal Nuhu, my faithful correspondent from Yardaje village; a friend of his, whom I do not recognize; and a chauffeur sent by Alhaji Moutari Aliyu, a village boy who has made it big. From humble origins in Yardaje, Moutari Ali now runs Tropical Motors in Kano, an import-resale business of used automotive vehicles.

Ground transportation would be quite smooth in Africa were it not for four constraints: availability, reliability, comfort, and safety. In Niger I had grown accustomed to sharing my travel quarters in open-back trucks with live animals; in Nigeria I was used to entrusting my fate to crazed and speeding taxi drivers who delighted in playing chicken with oncoming traffic on the open highway. Indeed, after one particularly harrowing trip, I could not resist looking the maniacal driver in the eye and grimly prophesying—even as he laughed—"You will die. If you keep driving like this, that is how you will die." How, then, would I bring my son upcountry to the border villages?

It was the one logistical detail I could not work out in advance. The times I had used a series of collective taxis from the "auto market" in Kano, the trip used to take minimum of four hours; mishaps, breakdowns, or unscheduled stops along the way had, on occasion, doubled the journey time. Once, on a late Friday afternoon, I was stuck eight miles from home in Zango, with bleak prospects of finding a vehicle before dark. A station wagon suddenly pulled up, heading toward Yardaje. Driver and passengers looked unusually grim: ordinarily, a white face animated most moods.

"*Babu wuri.* There is no room." I didn't quite understand. In bush taxis you can always find another few inches to squeeze in. For sure, the front cabin was bursting at the seams with passengers. Perhaps they assumed that, as a White Man, I would only accept to travel in a seat in the front.

"*Ba komi,*" I chimed in cheerfully. "That's all right. I'll get in the back." There seemed plenty of room there. No passengers, even, just a big box.

"You won't be comfortable there," said the driver.

Comfort? This was a most unusual consideration. Why didn't the driver want to take me on as a paying passenger? What was going on? Only my persistent obtuseness drove the driver into a rare attempt at tact.

"There's a corpse in there."

I peered again. The "big box" was, indeed, a coffin. Recently filled, too, from all appearances. The glum folk in the front, I now understood, were next of kin.

I am not superstitious. I am no necrophobe, and I desperately wanted to be home in my hut before dark. But all my sojourns in Hausaland have been premised on bending to local customs, and insisting upon riding in the back of a vehicle next to an in-use coffin hardly qualified as culturally appropriate.

Now I am realizing a dream by bringing my son back with me into the heart of Hausaland. But at the same time, I know that there are certain experiences from which I must shield Sam. Avoiding cadavers as travel companions is not as critical as avoiding nighttime travel, when ordinary road fright becomes outright nightmarish. We will need to spend our first night in the big city. It is the one leg of the trip I fear most and can control the least.

Besieged by petulant porters and beggars as we leave the terminal, we unwittingly become the objects of hilarity. Wanting to demonstrate to Sam my position on alms-giving and tipping, I offer a few kobo—Nigerian coins—to a boy leading his blind father and give some naira—paper money—bills to the airport hanger-ons who have carried our luggage to the waiting car. Previous visits had taught me what amounts were appropriate, and I was quite prepared for these touchdown transactions: squirreling away the local currency for succeeding trips is an entrenched habit. From a financial point of view I always like to hit a foreign country running, without having to begin the journey with moneychangers. This time, I had even distributed some of my leftover coin of the realm to Sam.

The beggars, the porters, even my hosts look at our distributions tactfully, in quiet incredulity. In the car I explain that, in preparation for my eventual return, I had carefully set aside this money from my last trip to Nigeria over a decade before. My hosts break out into raucous laughter. "*Naira ya fadi kwarai!* How has the naira fallen!"

Inflation has so run its course that the lowest denomination of currency is now the twenty naira bill, the equivalent of about twenty cents.

My ten, five, and one naira bills—which had once been quite useful for minor transactions—are now completely useless. Coins had become extinct. My hosts howl at the image I have just presented to the beggars and the porters, we rich American visitors, just off the plane, blithely distributing antiquated currency and mistaking the gesture as largesse. To the recipients of our grants, our conduct has not been miserly so much as just plain weird. From what planet had we descended? From what time warp? For Sam, it was a fitting introduction to the African economy.

I needn't have worried what kind of imposition my initial request to stay over at Moutari Ali's own home would present. The village-boy-made-good—whose late father I had befriended during my original village research—is putting us up at the Kano hotel of our choice.

We choose the premier class Daula Hotel, whose tantalizing swimming pool unfortunately nurtures an unwelcome species of patron: the mosquito. Recalling that mosquitoes are completely absent from the bush during the cold season, back in New England I had eschewed the prescribed malarial pills for Sam and me; I had forgotten, however, that in the city mosquitoes *are* a year-round bane. They harass us all night long.

A knock at the door. Ten o'clock, eleven? Where are we? I open the door and a couple of excited Nigerians enter the cramped room. I am supposed to recognize them but I do not. One of the visitors, a strapping young man, keeps grinning and speaking to me in rapid-fire Hausa. He apparently is one of the countless young boys I had befriended fourteen years before. Although all grown up now, he still relates to me as if I were the Mallam Beel of yesteryear, the Pied Piper of his youth. Sam does not stir. They stare at my sleeping progeny.

It is precisely the scenario I had foreseen with dread: reuniting with old acquaintances whom I can no long recognize, perhaps not even remember. Pretending that I *do* know them. Faking it. Failing at resurrecting my Hausa self .

Who had that Mallam Beel been? A strange White (and therefore wealthy) Man who lived in a mud hut like everyone else, spoke Hausa like a "Kano donkey" (a true compliment!), and rode his own horse around the village, through the bush, and across the border. The playful foreigner whose everyday stroll through the village, even after months of residence, would trigger throngs of children following and delightfully squealing, "Mallam Beel! Mallam Beel!" Was that the same person as this middle-aged man, now ensconced in a pricey city hotel with a child of his own, a white boy to whom he ministered in a most un-African manner and with whom he communicated in the "European" language that some villagers swore he had forgotten entirely?

It is already happening, and we haven't yet returned to the village. We haven't even spent our first full night in Africa, and already I am playing miserably at being who I once had been.

We are received by Alhaji Moutari Aliyu in his palatial city home in the morning. Having been the pasha of Yardaje for so long, I find it strange suddenly to become the humble guest of this "son of the village." But I am grateful. With Moutari's car and driver, we can navigate the city market to secure the supplies necessary for a ten-day sojourn in the rural villages: mattress, fly net, kerosene stove, foodstuffs (rice, pasta, couscous), and bottled water.

The latter is a major concession: the seasoned dweller in rural Africa treats the local water himself; the macho one drinks it straight. It grieves me to spend as much money on a liter of H_2O as a villager earns in a day. But for Sam, whom I have just transported from one of the most secure environments in the world to one of the least, I must reduce the risks. "And you will not let him eat any meat, either," his anxious mother had commanded, her dark eyes vividly reflecting the memory of flies swarming around the Hausa butcher stalls we had frequented as a childless couple. Herein lay the yin-yang of bringing our only son on an equestrian mission to Hausaland: macrocosmic danger, microcosmic protection.

To shop, Sam and I need new naira. A bank? That's for foreigners, those with no connections, who don't know how to conduct business locally. Moutari Aliyu gets on the telephone and calls his favorite money changer.

"We have some visitors," he explains in Hausa, by way of introduction, "and they need to change some foreign money. How much for a dollar, U.S.?"

Pause.

"Only 104? Last week when I changed it was 102!"

In 1980, when I first arrived in Nigeria, you had to pay nearly two dollars for the naira. Unofficially, you could get a couple of naira for a single dollar, but you had to be careful. Now, a single naira is worth less than a penny, and on our behalf Moutari Aliyu is vigorously bargaining on the phone to determine *how* much less than a cent.

"All right, then," concludes Moutari, "but I'd better not find out that there is a better rate in the town marketplace." On the other end of the line comes reassurance: his is the just rate.

A short while later arrives Alhaji Moneychanger, in long robe and deep pockets. I open my wallet and carefully pull out three crisp Benjamin Franklins and one Ulysses S. Grant. He, in turn, plunks down three enormous, sand-gritty piles of faded twenty naira bills. Stacked one on top of the other, they measure over two feet tall. Sheer storage, if not financial security, is now an added concern: how does one discreetly lug three hundred dollars worth of money in twenty cent notes? We are left with a dusty plastic bag.

Sam, though, is ecstatic. When we convert his allocated ten dollars of spending money into naira, he literally has fistfuls of cash. Flush with wealth, he unsuccessfully tries stuffing his windfall into a snakeskin change purse.

At the city market in Kano—an outdoor jamboree of boisterous venders, squawking marketgoers, and jumbled traffic—Sam experiences for the first time the unpleasant sensation of being stared at.

"Why are they all looking at me?" he asks, for the first of a thousand times.

"They're just curious," I reply matter-of-factly. "They're not used to seeing people of our color. And they're certainly not accustomed to seeing white kids."

"It's rude," Sam retorts, rather judgmentally. "What's the big deal about being another color?"

"Well," I try explaining, this time presenting the concept of novelty. "It's like you're a miniature White Man, something they've never seen before."

"Still, I wish they'd stop looking at me all the time like that."

6

It is Friday afternoon, the Muslim sabbath. The road trip from Kano has taken only a couple of hours, including stops in the capital of the emirate, Daura. Here, according to ancestral legend, the original seven Hausa nations first emerged after a valiant prince from Baghdad slew the *dodo*, a fearsome, water well–obstructing dragon. As reward, the Queen of Daura married the prince; their son, together with his six sons, established the "legitimate" Hausa Seven dynasties. An equal number of sons, sired by the Persian prince with a concubine, founded "Seven Bastard" families. My heir and I stop in Daura merely to pay homage to the emir in his palace and to donate books to the public library.

Twelve miles to the east of Daura, along the asphalt highway, lies Zango. For the second half of the century following the Fulani jihad of 1805–7, Zango constituted the capital-in-exile of the royal Daura diaspora. In 1906, however, the British abolished the "decadent" Fulani dynasty and restored the Hausa to Daura. We stop briefly in Zango to ask for my old friend the petrol dealer, Gambo Mai-Mai.

A further eight miles east of Zango we arrive at the junction to Yardaje. We turn off the paved road and pause. I stare ahead, son by my side, at the same unpaved, dusty, bone-rattling, three-mile ordeal of a laterite track—snaking past the same denuded, rocky hills—over which my body first jostled in February 1983. I had no child, then, not even a wife. For that inaugural visit, I was accompanied by Souleymane Abba, a marabout friend with a lifelong disability, whom I'd known from the late 1970s . . .

No doubt about it: when Souleymane and I first showed up, unannounced, we constituted a veritable freak show for the amazed inhabitants of Yardaje. Either one of us, alone, would have been a curiosity in his own right: I for my color; he for his deformity. Arriving together, we created an out-and-out sensation.

As a scholar of Islam in a town that was still largely illiterate, Souleymane approached me, the high school teacher, as a peer, practically a colleague. He evinced neither the discreet deference nor defensive mockery that, in initial encounters, Muslim Black Africans often display toward the unknown White Man. As a scholar, a man of the book, Mallam ("Teacher") Souleymane assumed—correctly—that we would naturally understand each other. His respect for my secular *boku* (book) learning was matched by self-confidence emanating from advanced Koranic studies.

Apart from his ample lips, Souleymane's facial features, ebony in color, were fine, smooth even. His large brown eyes—often blinking and darting out of reflexive curiosity—bespoke keen intelligence. His head (on account of big brains?) appeared a bit larger to me than usual, but not aberrantly so. The most remarkable feature about Souleymane's face was his mouth: unlike most of his fellows, who suffered in various degrees from kola nut decay, Souleymane had teeth of an impeccable, pearly white. When he flashed them in laughter, the combination of penetrating pupils and brilliant smile conveyed a palpable impression of wisdom-cum-kindness. There was only one overt peculiarity about my amiable and erudite African friend: he got around by walking on his hands.

As a result of a childhood polio shot gone awry, Souleymane's legs were useless sticks: brittle, unbendable, pathetically thin limbs. To "walk," he would swing himself forward on handheld wooden blocks with his muscular arms and torso, landing on his knees at every "step."

Souleymane's common nickname, although never uttered with malice, made me wince every time I heard it: *Gurgu*, "The Cripple."

Shortly before I left Niger as a Peace Corps Volunteer in 1979, Harry Politopolous, a Greek economist working in Niamey for the United Nations, told me about Caritas, a Catholic relief agency with a local branch office. Not long after I wrote on my friend's behalf, Souleymane received his Third World wheelchair: a specially designed, hand-propelled, three-wheeler fitted with bicycle chain technology at outstretched arms length. I later learned that the local government—still under military regime—transferred the *keke* to Souleymane in a formal handing-over ceremony, during which I was undeservedly thanked..

On account of the difficulty of transporting it, in his rare excursions outside of Magaria Souleymane was reduced to "walking" in the pre-*keke* mode. So it was when we arrived together, the first time for both of us, in Yardaje. Souleymane had endorsed this prospective fieldwork site, over the border in Nigeria, because his wife had a relation living there, a tall, wiry, primary schoolteacher who spoke in a high-pitched, unintentionally sarcastic tone. His name was Murtalla. Murtalla called Souleymane, Mallam Abba.

Although it was Murtalla who, after the proper introductions and explanations, led us to the chief—Holder-of-the-Village, Head-of-the-District, King-of-the-Fulani, the Pilgrim-to-Mecca Harou—it was the spectacle of Souleymane and me heading toward the adobe palace that arrested the attention of my future hosts and neighbors. "Gurgu da Bature!" whooped the children, skipping in delight. "Gurgu da Bature!"

In English, to speak of "the blind leading the blind" is derisive indeed. In Hausaland, however, where it is not uncommon for the sightless to travel about in tandem, maintaining rank by holding on to each other's shoulders or to opposite ends of a stick, a literal translation carries no parallel opprobrium. With "Gurgu da Bature," though, we begin to get at a more culturally apposite—and ludicrous—image: "Cripple and White Man!" the kids were shrieking hysterically. "A Cripple and a *White* Man!"

Thus did I make my first appearance in Yardaje, seventeen years before.

"That's the schoolhouse!" I point out excitedly to Sam, when we reach the outskirts of the village. My son looks at the unadorned, cinderblock structure, and I can tell from his deadpan face what he is thinking: This is nothing at all like my school back home.

There is no raucous greeting as I'd anticipated: little children look curiously at our van but, with the windows rolled up for air conditioning, cannot easily see inside. Even if they could see, what would they know to think? All these children have been born since my departure. A new Pied Piper awaits creation.

Sanoucou! That means "greetings" in Hausa . . . When we arrived, we made a huge sensation. Everyone *was surprised to see me, and acted like I was a miracle. I'm not too surprised. I wasn't born last time dad was here, and after all, I am the son of the "legendary" hero Mallam Bill.*

Sam and I are ushered into the antechambers of the chief's palace, an adobe structure with dirt floor, and issued straw mats. Our chief, Alhaji Harou—"holder of the village," district head, and King of the Fulanis—is still at prayer in the mosque in the village square.

The antechambers are soon crowded with curious kids, royal and not, staring at us in utter amazement. Sam retreats into a posture that he will often adopt during these next ten days: reaching into his leather-skinned Koran holder, he extracts his diary book with a *République du Niger* map on the cover—the very same school notebook I had assiduously saved since being gifted with it in 1979—and begins writing . . .

Right now, I'm in the chief of the village's reception room. I'm being stared at by about 7 African children. I'm wondering, What is so interesting about a (white) American boy writing in a journal? All they're doing is leaning on the inside wall of the house and staring . . . Oh, no, a billion more kids are coming to stare!

From the same holy book bag, Sam whips out and consults his well-worn copy of *Treasure Island.*

"Mallam Beel, greetings on your return!" exclaims the spectacled chief, as he returned from prayer.

"Greetings unto you!" I reply.

"How was your journey?"

"It passed in health."

"How was your family when you left them?"

"Alhamdu lillahi," I answered in prayer-greeting. "Praise be to Allah."

"How is Loïza? And your 'old lady'?"

"Both in health," I replied, gratified to recall both feminine and plural pronoun forms for my wife and mother.

"How are your brothers? And Eliyu, your friend who came here and visited with you?"

"All in health." The chief is too diplomatic to use Elly's local nickname, The Bearded One.

"And how have the years treated you since we were last separated."

"We thank God."

"How many years has it been?"

When I told him, the chief uttered a sound that was somewhere between a *tsk* and a gasp.

"And Arielle? In health?"

It is truly an honor that the chief recalls the name of our firstborn, a girl. When our daughter was born I mailed instructions to Taigaza, the town crier, that he should canvass the village and belt out the good news. Two years after Arielle's birth I'd returned for a very short visit, distributing pictures.

"And your son?"

"Here he is," I exclaim, as proud as any Hausa father, stepping to the side so that the King of the Fulanis can see my backward-baseball-cap-wearing son, scribbling away in his notebook.

"He is the one that Loïza gave you after your departure?"

"It is indeed he."

Now it is the chief's turn to invoke the deity. "Ikon Allah!" he exclaims. "Power of God!"

My dad is keeping a journal, also. He had it last time he was in Africa. On the cover, it says "June 1989" and then "February 2000 (with Sam!)" The next time I go to Africa, I'll also dig this journal up and use it as my official Africa Journal.

Although our horse problem in the neighboring village has nothing to do with the people here, it would be unthinkable to bypass Yardaje for the sake of expeditious problem-solving in Yekuwa. During over a year of prior residence, I had carefully ensured that neither village felt slighted vis-à-vis the other by always allotting the identical number of nights to each. We cannot do differently now—especially since the chief of Yardaje has provided us accommodations within his own palace.

I was excited to see the house in which we would sleep in Yardaje, because it looked like the adobe houses in my Social Studies book. It was made of sun baked clay and had a metal door. The whole "domain" we would live in, including the walls, was practically 100% clay. Cool.

Though royal in name, there is nothing grandiose about our quarters. Passing a corrugated aluminum door (with a latch just big enough to fit a suitcase lock and key), we enter a covered, dark, three-sided adobe-walled antechamber with beaten earthen floor. From inside the antechamber we can slide shut a latch, ostensibly to secure the door.

Turning right, we exit the antechamber and find ourselves in the open air, with a six-foot-high inner adobe wall on our left; to our right, just a few feet away, is an even higher mud-caked wall, the one separating the compound from the dirt-brown street.

After about ten paces the inner wall ends and we turn left through a portal that leads us into the spacious courtyard of hard, brown earth. Ahead of us stands our sleeping quarters: a one-room adobe hut, fitted with a corrugated aluminum door so small I need to bend to enter, and two cut-out windows with scrap iron bars. Inside: nothing. Nothing except for philosophical graffiti chalked on one wall by the hut's former high school student occupants. Soon, though, the chief thoughtfully provides us with "furniture": one enormous plastic mat that covers most of the floor.

Except for about 3 feet in front of the "house" the ground was soil, sand, and rock. This I had expected. The 3 feet in front of the house was concrete. That was surprising because I didn't think there was concrete anywhere except in the cities . . .

Someone is nailing in our door to place a lock on it. This place is so dusty, when you hit the wall you suddenly find dust in your hair and eyes. See ya later!

To one side of the compound, concealed by an adobe wall but also open air, is the toilet: a slightly raised cement mound with a hole. Judging from the seconds between bodily evacuation and dull thud, the latrine must be at least ten yards deep. It is behind this wall that Sam and I will take our "Hausa baths," dipping a plastic cup into a big pot, pouring it over one another, and in turn soaping each other's back. For luxury's sake during this cold season, I will preheat the water on our kerosene stove. I will also teach Sam the secret of the Hausa bath: if you crouch during the pouring, the water does not bounce back and splatter you with ground dirt. Crouching for my baths and bowel movements will remind my forty-four-year-old joints, however, of the Peace Corps forester with bad knees who would have been medevaced home had he not secured a specially fitted outdoor latrine toilet seat. Once upon that time, it impressed me enormously that the Peace Corps would pay for a custom-fit excretion throne. Nowadays I am scandalized by stories of exploitative Volunteers successfully insisting on expensive beds and mattresses, reputedly on account of "aggravated back problems" but really because they just want the most comfortable sleeping arrangements they can get Uncle Sam to subsidize.

For our part, Sam and I will sleep on the floor of our hut on the mattresses we purchased in Kano. More against flies than mosquitoes, we string nets around the mattresses; for the same reason, we hire the village carpenter to nail our unfurled, Home Depot–purchased insect screens onto the windows and door casing. A few hanging rolls of gooey fly tape—which will periodically get stuck to my hair—and voilà: our humble homestead (actually quite extravagant by local standards) is now complete.

If I take pains to describe these temporary living quarters in Yardaje, it is to explain better the various precarious lines of defense in the constantly breached fortress of privacy that I have attempted to construct for my son. For if Sam felt uncomfortable being stared at in the relative urbane environment of Kano, in the villages he has instantly become a veritable zoo attraction: the miniature White Man on public display!

I'm now in our new room (being stared at, of course) on my new mattress. I have a wallet stuffed with a lot *of money. My dad had that wallet 13 years ago. He also had the goatskin bag I use for the markets . . .*

Some men have come to say hello again, though when the adults open the gates, it gives a chance to the kids to slip in. Darn. Now they're staring again. By the way, everyone who meets me wants to shake my hand, and, of course,

I have to. They ask me a ton of questions in Hausa ("How's Loïza? How are you?") A lot of times the answer is: "Lafia Lo (La-FEE-A-LO) which means "good/fine!!"

For the children of Yardaje the outer wall of our compound serves as a peering perch. Similarly, the closed door of the antechamber constitutes a frank invitation for the nimble and wiry to crawl and squeeze through the tiny space between bottom frame and door post. The portal of the inner wall provides only the most temporary of lookout posts from which wide-eyed kids stare at us across the courtyard: soon enough, they will be at the actual door of our hut, gazing in wonder through the fly-screen door flap. But when the juvenile throng grows thick, those at the front are inevitably pushed forward, traversing the flimsy screen and doorjamb. (If an adult is ushered into our hut, this also becomes a tacit signal for the bolder of the children to come in.) Only the very last defense post is immune from actual infiltration. From its perimeter, through the tiny holes stitched together in white fabric, one can see the exotic creature: pink-skinned Sam, under a bed net, book or diary in hand. But more than the physical cloth barrier, Sam's ultimate refuge and escape from the discomfort of non-stop gawking derives from the act of reading.

For all of my 10 days, dad says I'll be stared at. Heaven help me! I think I'm going to die of embarrassment.

Early morning provides temporary respite from the geek show that so bothers my son. In the cold season dawn we have only one regular visitor: Hassan, "King of the Workers," son of the village chief, and cow tender par excellence.

"Mallam Beel, The One Who Belongs to Loïza, did you sleep well?"

I invariably do sleep well in Hausaland.

"How is the cold?"

"It's time for it."

"Samuel is in health?"

"We thank Allah."

Hassan, still sturdy and ever smiling, has always been one of my closest friends in Yardaje, a straightforward soul whose unbounded zest for life has never been complicated by formal education or literacy. It is perhaps because Hassan can neither read nor write that there is so little awkwardness about our reuniting: no vague unease about the lack of communication over the intervening years, only the spontaneous joy between souls for whom human relationships *can* only be face-to-face. If you have friends with whom you communicate only by telephone, youthful chums with whom you only exchange New Year's cards, acquaintances whom you "know" only through e-mail, or "conference colleagues" whom you see only at annual conventions, then you know the awkwardness of personal get-togethers that rupture the regular mode of contact. There is no other way that I can be with Hassan than like this: returning to his home village, even after the lapse of a decade.

For Hassan, Sam delights in making an additional cup of morning tea from our Kano-bought, Chinese-made, kerosene stove: soaking the cotton-tipped metal lighter in kerosene, lighting it with a match, and then getting the cotton strands around the base of the stove to catch fire. It is a big person's job and Sam loves performing it. For Hassan, Sam pours in awe even more sugar than my sweet-toothed son does for himself, adding until our guest finally says *shi ke nan*—that's it, no more.

Sugar is a luxury item in the African bush, and I have to explain to Sam that glucose excess is not the reason for the lamentable dental state in which so many of our Hausa friends find themselves.

"Then why are they missing so many teeth, Dad?"

"They chew kola nuts, Sam. It's the kola nuts that hurt their teeth and give them that red color."

"Then why do they do it?"

"Why do you eat so much candy if you know it's not good for you?"

Tooth loss is indeed the most obvious sign of aging that, after a decade's absence from the village, I notice. It is a poignant reminder that conventional indices of underdevelopment rarely include *access to dentists*, even though the quality of one's life is so intimately tied to the health of one's teeth. It also makes me acutely aware that, deep down, I too harbor a vulgar stereotype, instinctively associating missing teeth with witlessness. Why, indeed, does our Western culture lead us to link intelligence with dentine?

Hassan has always been my guide into the furthest corners of local culture. On the chief's farm he taught me how to plant millet seed (in a kind of barefoot dance shuffle you make a depression in the sand with your left foot, drop a handful of seeds in the hole, and then cover it again with the right foot). Hassan taught me Hausa hand symbols, which so many years later still cause me cross-cultural confusion: rolling an index finger on the side of the head, which to Americans signifies craziness, is the Hausa sign for royalty (on account of the wrapped turban that chiefs wear on their head); bending the fingers on both hands, which Jews do next to a lit braided candle in the ritual marking the end of the Sabbath, in Hausa sign language connotes leprosy; tapping your forehead with extended right index finger, in alignment with your nose, means "absolutely delicious" (with respect to food and women alike).

It is with Hassan that I used to discuss sexual relations, both among married and non-married folk; and it was to me that Hassan came in uncharacteristic anger one day, telling me to formalize, in writing, the divorce that he had spontaneously decided upon after his wife had just refused to serve him a proper meal and stalked off to her parents' home. (Despite my attempts at counseling a cooling-down period, I succumbed to my friend's beseechments and wound up transcribing the Muslim formula "I divorce her, I divorce her, I divorce her," thereby dissolving the marriage.)

In the past Hassan would come to me for medical treatment, an old habit into which we now easily relapse. This time his leg is infected, probably due to a thorn that stuck into his shin while he was weeding, barefoot and with upturned trousers.

"Why didn't you go to the dispensary doctor" I ask in deliberate naïveté, "instead of waiting all this time for me to return from America?"

"Because there's no medicine like Mallam Beel medicine." It has been a long time since I've dealt with oozing puss, antibacterial ointments, and stretch bandages. Is it good for my son to watch me practice medicine without a license? But this is not the major crisis of medical conscience that this trip has occasioned. Nor is it the decision to bring my son into a tropical disease zone, particularly during meningitis season. My pangs of medical guilt rather converged most intensely at the pharmaceutical desk at Rhode Island Memorial Hospital where the receptionist asked me pointblank, "How many do you want?"

It was thanks to the Internet and our Jewishly pious pediatrician, Joshua Gutman—a former Peace Corps Volunteer himself—that I'd tracked down the only commercially available bulk source of oral rehydration. These relatively inexpensive packets have long been prescribed by the World Health Organization as the cheapest, most effective way of saving Third World babies from death by diarrhea. Previous sojourns had taught me how painfully common diarrheal death among infants is in Yardaje and Yekuwa; indeed, I had once been ecstatically transported by being handed an hours-old newborn by her father, my census assistant in Yekuwa, only to be later plunged into depression to hear him murmur, after I asked about his daughter's health, "Ta raisuwa"—she'd passed away.

So although the major purpose of our journey is to untangle a horse knot, shouldn't my son and I also save baby lives along the way? Indeed, how can we travel to a place of such high infant mortality and *not* pack along some of those lightweight ORT kits?

It's a simple case of Morality 101—until you realize that the hospital receptionist's simple question "How many do you want?" actually translates into "How many babies' lives are you prepared to save?" You then find yourself on that slippery and guilt-wracked slope of insufficient liberalism, knowing that any amount of baby-saving ORT you bring along will still be insufficient, and that there will always be one more village baby dying of simple diarrhea even if you stuff your suitcases with nothing *but* ORT packets. You also can't help confronting the true limits of your generosity: How much of my personal travel and entertainment budget—not to mention life savings—am I willing to spend on baby saving, anyway? What is the right amount of monetary sacrifice to make in a land where infant death is inevitable, recurrent, and seemingly eternal? Is it moral to travel to these parts for any other reason than to save innocent lives? Why travel there at all, when philanthropy can be just as easily—and much more cheaply—provided from afar?

I have to remind myself: I am not merely another white, middle-class liberal with vague sympathies for Third World babies. I am Mallam Beel/Mista Bello, a quasi-African on a specific horse-recovery mission with his rightful heir. Everybody can understand the ethics of this journey in Hausaland, even if in America nobody can.

In Jewish mysticism eighteen is a propitious number, for its characters literally spell out *chai*, the Hebrew word for life. Multiples of eighteen are proportionately auspicious. Faced in the Rhode Island clinic with choosing how many hypothetical Hausa babies to save from future death by diarrhea, I transcend indecision by calculating a double *chai*, multiplying by two (one for each village), and plunking down the odd number of greenbacks to procure a Kabbalistically based rate of reduced infant mortality.

Love at first horse: the author, as Peace Corps Volunteer in Magaria, with Iska ("Wind").

Mamane Alassane, housekeeper for Peace Corps Volunteers, with wife Ladi and children, c. 1979.

Two decades later: Mamane as grandfather.

Object of the author's first African livestock imbroglio: Bange, mounted by Lawali, the intended beneficiary.

Sarkin Harou, chief of Magaria district (Niger), to whom the author ultimately appealed for judgment.

Courtesy visit to the Emir of Daura (Nigeria),
Alhaji Muhammadu Bashar. Prior to the colonial partition,
Daura ruled over many settlements in present-day Niger.

(opposite) The author with the chief of Yardaje
and his sons Ibrahim (left) and Hassan (right).

With secondary school teacher Lawal Nuhu, Yardaje's first university graduate.

With the district chief of Yekuwa, Bachir Harouna, son of the chief of Magaria.

Alhaji Aminu, village chief of Yekuwa-Kofai.

Sam with the family of Mallam Souleymane (left), Islamic teacher and the author's friend from Peace Corps days in Magaria.

Alhaji Mallam Harouna, Islamic teacher and steadfast friend in Yekuwa.

Faralu, the author's groom in Yekuwa, tasting Passover fare.

"King of the Tea Men" of Yekuwa (Jamilu aka Mansour) with a gift packet of tea leaves from Mauritius.

Accommodations in Yekuwa.

Survival storage: stocking the granary after the harvest

The author and Faralu with horse reimbursement money.

Representative of the Blindmen's Village Council receives horse purchase witness money.

Horse problem resolved:
Sam meets the new Sa'a
for the first time.

Yekuwa lass.

Sam being fitted out by Jagga, the town crier.

On the borderline: Sa'a "heads" into Nigeria, while Sam is still in Niger.

Fulani women greet Sam outside of Yekuwa as he sets off back to America.

Farewell serenade for chief of Yardaje,
Alhaji Harou, "King of the Fulani."

7

The people were interested in me probably because I looked different, with white skin and lots of hair. I had less interest in them because I had seen black people all the time, while they had never seen a white person before. The kids probably didn't have a good education, or just didn't think I was a real kid and didn't have feelings. They just kept on touching my hair, my skin, etc. They would always surround us and follow dad and I wherever we went. God, could those kids stare! It made me feel on-stage, or in-the-spotlight, with all that attention.

Hassan is one of the few people in Yardaje to whom I confide my horse problem in nearby Yekuwa, as well as my uncertainty about how to proceed. He already seems to have an inkling about the matter but exercises characteristic discretion. I do not want to let on that I have returned solely on account of the horse; even less do I wish for people in Yardaje to think that I am badmouthing their counterparts in Yekuwa.

"You're not the one who should bring it up," Hassan counsels me in Hausa. "Just be patient. Let those of the late chief's family raise the matter."

"But what if they don't? What if they don't say anything about it."

"Then you merely say, after a day or so, 'Hey, I feel like riding my horse now. Where is it?'" Hassan chuckles at his own suggested subterfuge, so effective for all its transparent ingenuousness.

Surely, all the concerned parties in Yekuwa must have known of my correspondence with Alhaji Mallam Harouna. Could I possibly feign ignorance of the horse heist? Hassan has usefully reminded me of the necessity for considerable tact and indirection, at least in the initial stages of the horse probe. But the *hak'uri* and *hankali*, the patience and wile, normally required for problem fixing in Hausaland usually come with an elastic timeframe: you wait, you discuss, you argue for as long as it takes until either coming to a mutual understanding or submitting to equally lengthy arbitration. But Sam and I do not have the ordinary luxury of unlimited time. Once we arrive in Yekuwa, we will have only three and a half days. Worse, I don't even have a game plan.

Sa'a, the horse, is not the only treasure I had left behind. In each of the villages I'd left behind a trove of household, first aid items, and climatically apposite clothes, confidant that I would need them in the not too distant future. (Bulky items, such as chairs, beds, and mattresses, I'd distributed as long-term loans.) In Yardaje, I left my possessions in a metal trunk that I'd entrusted to Lawali, my schoolteacher friend.

The last time Dad had been in Africa, he buried all his belongings in a chest and gave the key to the lock to a friend. Now, 16 years later, the Lawali person still has the key. We dug the chest up and found useful things: blankets, pillows, gas lamps, pots, pans, spoons, cooking utensils, etc. We had full use of it, so I took a thick blanket (because at night and morning it's a little cold), got warm and slept.

In America, the paltry contents of our "buried" treasure would have made for a poor yard sale, even if Sam's "etc." also includes drinking cups and glasses, water purification pills, bandages, flashlights, gas canisters, old shirts, and sneakers. There are even some miniature plastic animals: my previous departure had been so chaotic (but aren't they always?) that I hadn't the opportunity to properly distribute all the toys. All these years I'd lived without the contents of the treasure chest, and could have thoughtlessly survived forever without them; yet the trunk still contains more creature comforts than all the villagers combined possess in a lifetime.

In all of the village I have seen only two doors: ours and Lawali's. Our door looked like it was made out of aluminum. For a lock, it had two pieces of wood that were nailed down so that it could swing forward and backwards, making a crude lock.

Lawali's was a door of wood, the kind most Americans would call junk and throw away. Lawali and his family, however, thought otherwise; they leaned it against the doorway and supported it with a rock. They also used a rock as a "lock"; it just prevented people from coming into the house, which is what a lock is supposed to do.

Protocol demands that before leaving our home in Nigeria we pay a courtesy call on the emir. For decades Alhaji Muhammadu Bashar had been in charge of the emirate of Daura; it was he whose blessing I'd required in order to receive the actual hospitality of his "subjects" in the village, and who put me through my quasi-doctoral oral exam. For myself, the infinitely long waits in the antechambers before being received had always been unbearable. But for Sam, this will be a once-in-a-lifetime opportunity to be ushered into a real fairytale-like palace and be introduced to an actual king.

Buckingham Palace, even if more architecturally grandiose than the adobe minarets of the Sahel, does not have floridly bedecked retainers wearing turbans and swords who greet ten-year-old Little Leaguers as if they were themselves royalty. Nor do a coterie of retainers follow the queen, announcing her entrance at the top of their lungs. As it turns out the aging emir—wearing an elaborate turban knotted at the top like rabbit ears—did not receive (or did not remembering receiving) the letter I had sent in advance from America, announcing our planned arrival. But at home Sam had had an inadvertent peek at the draft, lying next to my printer:

January 9, 2000
His Royal Highness
Emir of Daura
B.P. 1
Daura
Katsina State
NIGERIA

Your Excellency,
Too many years have elapsed since I last visited Nigeria, Daura, and Yardaje. For that reason, I have decided to embark on a short visit of ten days' duration so as to reestablish face-to-face contacts with old friends. (There is also a small problem of inheritance in Yekuwa which I need to resolve.)

Moreover, I am bringing my son Samuel along with me. As they say in Hausa, *ya yi wayo* and it is time to introduce him to Hausaland.

If all goes well, we should be arriving from Kano on Friday, February 18. Although it is a day of prayer, I hope you will be available so that I may have the honor and pleasure of introducing you to my son for the very first time.

Sincerely,

"What does '*ya yi wayo*' mean?" Sam had asked, intrigued by the letter.

"Old enough to begin understanding the ways of the world," I explained.

"Is he really a king? I thought there weren't any real kings any more. Just those in storybooks."

"He's a real king," I insisted. "Emir, king, sultan—it's the same thing. He's the king of Daura. And it's always better to let royalty know in advance when you are going to pay them a call."

Hi. It's 12:30. I am now in the emir's palace in the waiting room. An emir is a king . . .

Hi again! It's 12:45. The King of Daura has arrived and everyone else has left. Dad is talking to the Emir (who speaks better English than anyone I know in Africa) about the books he had given the emir last time they had met. [On our way up from Kano] he gave those same books (except different copies) to the Library of Daura which was founded in 1950.

Everyone who speaks to the emir must first bow down (more like kneeling and touching the ground with their hands).

"I myself was on a trip to America not many months ago," the emir palavers in British-accented English, looking over what may have been the first white child to enter his royal chambers, "and I brought my grandchildren along. We thoroughly enjoyed Disneyworld. Now *that* is a wonderful place. Truly wonderful."

Had the emir visited Disneyworld in his royal robes and turban, I thought, onlookers would surely have assumed that he was one of the attractions. But I know that when he travels to Western countries his Highness dresses as a Westerner; in Orlando, he probably would have been taken for an ordinary retiree, the nondescript descendant of just another African slave from elsewhere in the South.

I shall never begrudge the old emir—for whom it must now be a chore to mount his royal horse at the end of Ramadan and parade through the streets of his capital—the pleasure of treating his grandchildren to the arcades, the theme parks, the glitz and the shlock of Americana. But for my own children I pray that Daura remain more wondrous than Disney, and that owning a horse in Hausaland thrill more than screeching down the Matterhorn.

For Sam, the highlight of Daura is neither entering the palace nor meeting the emir. More memorable is being handed wads of naira and having his name changed.

In Hausaland it is a custom to give your out-of-town visitor money, especially if he or she is less highly ranked than you. This is done primarily as a token of appreciation for the efforts expended in traveling, under presumably difficult conditions, just to see you; the money may often represent the visitor's sole source of return bus fare. I am more used to being on the giving side of this equation although on occasion, in extremely remote villages that I have been able to reach only on horseback, it is I who have been on the receiving end, eternally humbled as an impoverished peasant—whom I could not refuse without insulting—would hand me a gritty, threadbare bill from his precious life savings, the equivalent of twenty-five or fifty cents.

Samuel is naturally assimilated into this custom, one old Daura friend after another reaching into the folds of his gown to extract a fistful of naira for my son: five dollars worth, ten dollars worth . . .

Hi! I'm in a friend's house. The first person we visited, Alhaji Galadima Ya'u [the Yardaje chief's eldest son] *gave me a ton of Nigerian bills! The second, Alhaji Lawal* [who holds Daura's traditional title of "Town Hygiene Inspector"], *also gave me money. Again, I tried to refuse but he insisted. I got photographed by a professional that he had summoned to the house and hopefully we'll receive copies of the photo.*

Alhaji Lawal (who speaks English very fast) talked about how my dad is called Mallam Beel and Mistah Bello and Mallam Bello. I learned that in Hausa, even though people call me Samouel, my name would be SA-MA-ILA. He wanted me to write it in my journal. In Arabic, it is written like this . . .

. . . at which point Alhaji Lawal's handwriting appears in my son's journal. For the rest of the trip my son is—and, in these corners of Africa, for the rest of his life will continue to be—known as Sama'ila. Village friends who subsequently learn of the change do not take it lightly or as a joke: an indigenizing name change in the emirate's capital, particularly by a royal title holder, is viewed almost like a conversion.

Good morning! Yesterday we went for a walk. Soon the news spread and the whole village accompanied us. We saw someone eating sugar cane and because in Martinique I had tasted it, I knew I loved it. I was about to buy some with my own money when the sugar cane seller insisted on giving it as a gift. I enjoyed a sugary sugar cane all the way.

It wasn't very nice of the village children, but for some reason, they wanted to see what I felt like. People were constantly petting and feeling my neck and hair. I felt like an animal in a petting zoo.

Why have I transported my young son Samuel into the African bush? Yes, so that he be there in person to retrieve his Hausaland legacy, his African horse. Yet also so that he know my version of Africa up close, intimately, in wondrous naïveté. And, no less important, so that I repay my Hausa hosts with immediate, tangible, precious proof of my lifelong connection to, and trust, in them.

But now that we are actually here, what is it that my son most needs from me? Protection, isolation, privacy. He is overwhelmed by the attention he attracts, by the unrestrained hospitality, the untempered excitement, and the raucous goodwill that villagers wish to express. Why did I think it would be easier for a ten-year-old him than it was for a twenty-one-year-old me the first time I ventured into the hinterlands of Hausaland?

After the walk we had our dinner. On a camping stove about a foot wide and thick, we boiled water, and put in the spaghetti and tomato sauce we had bought in the city markets. It tasted weird. We had forgotten salt! As we had learned in Social Studies, in Africa salt is expensive. We bought two bags of salt for ten naira. With ten naira, you could buy a pack of batteries! (My dad was dumbfounded when I talked about Mali & Timbuktu trading gold for salt.)

In the evening, in response to my request, a woman appears in my courtyard: the widow of Alhaji Habou. Years before, when I received word by mail of Habou's fatal accident, I'd made a vow; now, finally, I am about to fulfill it.

Like the family of the chief of Yardaje village, Alhaji Habou was a Fulani, a "redskin" descended from a long line of nomadic herders. As with most Fulani, Habou lived outside of the village proper, in a tiny bush settlement consisting of a few small huts inhabited by his immediate family members. Alhaji Habou was a very successful cattle herder, an unpretentious bigshot with fine features and twinkling eyes. He was also a great joker, often dropping in at all hours of the evening and night and teasing me about either the color of my skin or my inability to speak his native tongue, Filanci. He was, in the Fulani way of things, very tactile, and during much of our conversation he'd hold my hand with his own strong but slender fingers.

"Mallam Beel. Beel, Mallam." Invariably, we would begin our greetings by deliberately reversing each other's name, a pattern that he'd initiated. "Teacher Bill. Bill, the Teacher."

"Alhaji Habou," I'd reply. "Habou, the Pilgrim to Mecca."

"Djam?"

"Djam simool."

Knowing that this would have exhausted my command of the Fulani language, Alhaji Habou would then throw more greetings my way and express mock disappointment over my abject lack of understanding. Regardless of how late into the night we'd yarn, he'd insist on returning home, on foot, to his remote *rigage*, or homestead.

I settled into my "bed." I had a hard time sleeping at first; the children were still awake and playing past 12:00 am (midnight). When I woke up, I was cold. I took a thick blanket from the buried chest, got warm, and slept.

Once upon a cold and foggy Harmattan, I'd ridden horseback all the way to Alhaji Habou's domain. The sandswept landscape was as bleak as the sky, with no other habitations in range. My host instructed his wife to provide me a refreshment, and she rushed to collect milk so fresh that it was still warm from the cow's udder. Now, well over a decade later, she remembered my visit in fine detail.

To Western ears, the circumstances surrounding Alhaji Habou's demise might sound mildly comical. One rainy season night my friend's roof simply caved in during a storm, killing him as he lay in bed. *Shi ke nan.* Finished. I often thought of my own leaky roof in Yardaje, the clumps of mud falling on me and—worse—soiling my research papers. That's all it takes to die in Hausaland: a heavy rain. It is one of the innumerable reasons why death is anticipated so matter-of-factly.

Mourning in Massachusetts, I wondered: What could I do for my deceased friend? It was then that I thought about the widow he'd left behind. Would he not have wished for me to somehow help her? When, or how, was secondary. If, after these many years, Alhaji Habou's widow were still alive and living in the Yardaje area (I correctly assumed that she would have remained unmarried), I would honor my friend's memory in the only way I knew how. One of the several envelopes in which I'd put aside money for special purposes bore this label: "My Fulani Friend's Widow."

Now, with the slight, elderly, bent woman draped in shrouds at the door of my guest quarters courtyard in the nighttime, I don't know where the envelope is. But it doesn't matter. Habou's widow is anxious about having been summoned to my hut. So I explain.

"You know, Alhaji Habou was my friend. A very good friend. And he was a good man."

"Yes, he was."

"I was used to him, he was used to me."

"So it was."

"When I learned of his passing, my heart was damaged. I wanted to do something for him. But do what?

"We have a custom," I continue, though not really quite certain who this "we" is or to what custom I am referring. "If a friend dies, we try to help those whom he has left behind."

As often occurs when speaking Hausa to remote herdspeople and nomads, especially female ones, I ceased to be understood. Unaccustomed to ever seeing white people, some rural folk assume that I can only speak in a foreign tongue. Already confused by her presence in my home, Habou's widow asks Lawali the schoolteacher what is going on. Lawali "translates," repeating what I have just said in Hausa.

I reach into the folds of my *ashera*, my open slit shirt with deep pockets, and fish out a fistful of twenty naira bills. "Take it," I say. "On account of him."

In the nighttime dark, Habou's widow can not see from across the courtyard what I have extracted from my pockets. Slowly, cautiously, she walks over. Her small and bony fingers touch mine as I make the offering. Recognizing what I have placed in her frail hands, she promptly collapses to the ground.

"No, don't cry," Lawali pleads, such displays in front of unrelated menfolk being exceedingly embarrassing. But her tears are already flowing, accompanied by mournful gasps of ambivalent emotions.

After Habou's widow recovers, her first words are not addressed to me, but to Lawali. "Does he"—"he," in this context, meaning the strange Bature, the White Man, "Does he eat millet pasta? How long will he remain in the village?"

"No, he's cooking for himself and his son," Lawali explains. "You need not prepare any food for them."

Repayment, thanks, dignity, reciprocity: all the Fulani widow can think of doing now is to cook our meals for the duration of our stay. But all she knows how to cook is millet—millet pasta dough, millet balls in sour milk, maybe even fried millet fritters. She must not misunderstand. She must not think that I have given her money to serve as our cook.

The next day, Alhaji Habou's widow reciprocates in the only other way she knows: dispatching one of her sons to show himself. To be there. To be seen. Making the effort to travel from your home—however distant— to that of another. Herein lies the heart of the Hausa way: one human being presenting himself, herself, to another. Person to person. Soul to soul.

In the morning dad had oatmeal (he could make it because of the foot-by-foot camping stove) and I made cereal with powdered milk. I then boiled water, put a tea bag in a small cup, poured the water into the cup and, of course, added three or four sugar cubes. (I silently reviewed all our science about dissolving.) It was delicious. The rooster was crowing in the crack of dawn and even now, at 9:00, they're still yodeling and crowing their heads off.

8

We have water bottles to drink from but when we wash our faces, we have a big jug called a tekunia. *Right now I'm wearing a backward hat (for my neck) and sunglasses (for my eyes). Pretty soon, we'll go to the reception or waiting room of the chief to offer the gift of a blue rug. See ya later!*

A wedding! There is little as exciting in village life as the combination of serious ceremonialism and boisterous celebration represented by a Hausa wedding. It is also one of the rare occasions in which there is some semblance of crowd control: hundreds of men sit on mats on the ground, clustered by rank and relationship. Children are kept away: this is adult business. (Not even women, including the bride, take part in the public marital proceedings.) In the cycle of village life, there is little to parallel the dignity and majesty of a wedding.

I rush to extract Sam from the hut. He doesn't want to face the public again today. He doesn't want to be pulled away from his books; but isn't this our lucky chance to see an African wedding? What is more, seated among the dignitaries—the chief, the priest, the visiting notables—he won't be surrounded, as usual, by hordes of people.

"No, Dad, I *don't* want to go! Why can't I just stay in inside? I hate going out. I can't stand it. It's too hot. They're always following me."

I plead. I cajole. I reason. I insist.

At this moment, I'm at a wedding procession. I'm still in the village and (as usual) I was "escorted" by all the kids. Not to be mean but they don't wash more than once a week. They attract flies.

Except for the yelling praise singer, there is hushed silence as we abandon the unofficial "escort" and finally walk alone along the wide street toward the dignitary mat. Several rows deep, men in begowned finery, from villages throughout the district, are seated on the ground on each side of the street. The *mai-gari*, the village chief, makes room on the mat for Sam. A high-level visiting Muslim priest addresses me in fairly good English. I share with him my illustrated Hausa dictionary. He points out the pictures and definitions to the chief.

The praise singer zeroes in on me and raises a clenched fist.

"Lion!" he screams in stylized Hausa. "European lion! You have traveled from afar! How rich you are, how powerful! Look, people, he has come all the way to Yardaje! Lion!!"

Does Sam know that, far from being screamed at and threatened, I'm being lauded and heralded?

Among the visitors from outside Yardaje, a familiar face, two familiar faces. The first I have no difficulty recognizing: Alhaji Aminu, the short, stout, roundfaced, gravelly-voiced brother of the deceased chief of Yekuwa. It is he who has replaced his brother to become the new chief of Yekuwa. It is he, I have anticipated all these months, with whom I must eventually resolve the horse problem. It is he who has triggered so many conflictual feelings: the erstwhile friend who my dark side suspects has, with the passage of time and accretion of power, betrayed me.

Alhaji Aminu, chief of Yekuwa, is not looking me in the eye. His greetings are not laced with smiles. I fear the worst. I inform him that I shall be arriving in Yekuwa *jibi*: two days hence.

Behind Alhaji Aminu, chief of Yekuwa, peers an older, but still familiar, face. "Greetings, greetings!" he belts out with a broad smile.

"*Barka kadai!*" I reply. "Return greetings upon you!"

"Greetings. Do you recognize me?"

Another dreaded moment of non-recognition. But never had I anticipated that my failure to identify an old acquaintance would occur in such a public setting, with hundreds of onlookers. The context is also disorienting: which village is he from? From which side of the border, even?

Frantically trying to conjure up my lists of villager names, my mind goes blank. I take a stab, guessing that, like the visiting Chief Alhaji Aminu, this man too must be from Yekuwa. I picked the wrong name.

"Uh unh," he says, shaking his head, his smiling fading. "No, I am Galadima."

Galadima. Of course! The chief's right hand man. His adviser, the official witness, the royal notary and notary public. He would have witnessed the horse handover. But I had failed to recognize him.

A man soon comes running to announce that the respective parents have exchanged the proper words: the wedding is consecrated. The congregated assembly quickly gathers itself up from the mats and ground and heads home.

Ceremony concluded, all semblance of crowd control also disappears. Inevitably, an impromptu retinue of curious kids immediately surrounds us, prompting me to adopt my familiar "protect Sam posture": encircling my son with my arm. Even as we walk home to the hut in this awkward stance and with a boisterous following of kids, my mind drifts to the troubling, initial reunion with the men from Yekuwa. It has not gone at all as I planned. I'd miffed my recognition test with Galadima. Alhaji Aminu's demeanor bothered me, too, reinforcing my suspicions: had he not averted his eyes when I looked at him questioningly?

I'm glad, though, that I have succeeded in extracting Sam from his self-imposed under-the-bed-net, inside-the-hut, behind-the-walls adobe cocoon. Thanks to the wedding, we had had a rare moment of order and calm in the streets of Yardaje.

I'm back home from the wedding how. It's so *annoying how those kids think it's okay to touch me like that. They call my name and take the freedom to pull my arms just to see what they feel like. You'd think I was an alien! I really* hate *the way they touch me, screaming "Sa-mou-uel! Sa-mou-el!" Geez!*

"Mallam Bill, you have a visitor." It was a call to which I'd increasingly grown—and groaned—used. We were like doctors on call during an epidemic, liable at any moment to be asked to tend, graciously and courteously, to any stranger off the street. Merely by showing ourselves, by exchanging a few words of greetings, we fulfilled our obligation. Refusing to appear would be to insult. But how draining these social demands could become! This particular call came just a few hours after the wedding. Sam was fiercely re-ensconced under his net.

I exited the door to our sleeping hut, crossed the courtyard, traversed the alley to the antechamber, and opened the outer door. There, standing discreetly twenty feet away, not moving, he stood in flowing gown: Alhaji Mallam Harouna, my faithful friend from sixteen years before, the preacher and priest from Yekuwa, my correspondent about the horse.

"*Tsibihani lilahi,*" I exclaimed, using a powerful, untranslatable homage to Allah. "Alhaji Mallam Harouna. It is you!"

"It is I."

We take each other by the arms, hugging Hausa style.

"You are well? In health?"

"I am in health."

"Loïza is in health?"

"Yes, my wife is in health."

"Arielle?"

"We thank Allah for her health?"

"What about Samouel?"

"Come see." We walk to the adobe hut.

I switch to "European." "Sam, please come outside. Somebody wants to see you."

My son groans in protest. "No, Dad. Not again."

"Just for a minute, Sam."

"Dad, you told me that after the wedding, I wouldn't have to go out again today!"

"We're not *going* out. Just come from the room so that my friend can see you. It's the man who is helping us about your horse."

Noise of book being thrown down; word "Fine" spat with unmistakable sarcasm.

"That is he? Your son with Loïza?"

"It is he."

My Muslim priest friend turns slowly to my only son. His tone—always measured—is even more deliberate than usual.

"Samouel," Alhaji Mallam Harouna pronounces distinctly, addressing my son. "*Kana lafiya?*"

"*Lafiya lau,*" my ten-year-old son replies effortlessly. "In health."

"Your mother is in health? Your sister too?" the mallam continues in Hausa.

"*Lafiya lau.*"

"How did your journey go?"

"*Lafiya lau.*"

Alhaji Mallam Harouna turns back to me. "Samouel is a capable boy," he pronounces in admiration. "He is even beginning to speak Hausa. This is good."

"He is making efforts," I reply. "But it isn't easy for him."

Alhaji Mallam Harouna shakes his head. "Of course it isn't easy. But it is the effort that counts."

"Thank you, Sam," I tell my son. "You can go back into the hut now."

Alhaji Mallam Harouna turns to business. "When are you coming to Yekuwa?"

"*Jibi.* The day after tomorrow."

"How will you travel?"

"I don't know yet."

"We will send a vehicle for you."

A vehicle? I am incredulous. When I last visited, there was not a single car in Yekuwa. All trucks were in Yardaje. Even men of high prestige like Alhaji Mallam Harouna would walk the eight miles between villages.

"How can that be?"

"Haven't you heard? There has been a change in government. We have democracy now."

The connection escapes me.

"We too have politics. We too have political parties. We too have a local government, just like in Nigeria."

"So?"

"The head of our party is your friend Jamilu, King of the Tea Sellers. Only now he is King of the Motorcars."

"How is that?"

"The party has provided him with a vehicle. What time will you be prepared to leave in the morning?"

On the eve of our departure for Yekuwa, I receive an unusual visit: Sarkin Makaho, King of the Blindmen of Yardaje, and his retinue. It is common for blind people in Hausaland to organize informal associations at the community level. According to the survey I'd conducted in 1986, there were 41 disabled persons in Yardaje, ten of whom were blind. (There were also nine deaf people, eight cripples, six lepers, and eight *mahaukata*, or "crazies." The idea of deliberately counting the disabled came from the British colonial censuses I'd stumbled on in northern Nigerian archives.)

"Mallam Beel, we have come to see you."

I have always harbored a special weakness for blind Hausa. They are the only Africans with whom I can speak in an indigenous language without being seen, literally, as a White Man. For sure, even the blind villagers think of me as a foreigner, as a stranger; but it is only to their ears. Their eyes do not perceive a person who, by virtue of color, hair, and clothes, is completely different from top to toe. Blind Hausa "see" me differently than do their seeing friends and family. Theirs is a singularly non-epidermic, non-racial view.

"We, the blind, have heard about the United Nations," Sarkin Makaho begins, seated on a mat after we have shaken hands. "We have heard about it on the radio. We have also heard that the United Nations assists blind people like us. We would like you to ask the United Nations to help us here in Yardaje."

No one who has lived or worked in Africa is a stranger to such appeals. If Caucasian, you are regarded as a representative to the world of the White Man; if American or European, you are a spokesman for Western society in its entirety.

What am I to say on behalf of the UN? "It does many things, this United Nations. Helping the blind may very well be one of them. I am not sure. But I am doubtful that I could get the UN to send someone here to the village, or to even take a special interest in it. For the United Nations does not know about Yardaje."

"Of course," the Blind King's companions agreed among themselves. "How could the United Nations know about Yardaje? How ever would they know about us here? We are not big enough, not important enough."

"I can make inquiries," I admitted. "But even more, I wish to make my own contribution to your association. How many are you?"

From the answer I calculate a sum divisible by a whole number and hand over an equivalent amount of naira. As is the custom, the King of the Blind has the money counted out publicly by a sighted companion.

"*Mun gode, mun gode*," he thanks me, as he stands up with the help of cane and companion's arm. "May Allah preserve us all."

"*Amin*," I respond. "Amen."

9

At the appointed time in the morning of the designated day, a battered Land Rover from Niger rumbles across the frontier into our village. It is under the direction of Jamilu, former King Teaman of Yekuwa, now King of the Motorcars.

Jamilu, whose birth name is Mansur but whom I always call "King Teaman," is always with a smile on his lips and joke on his tongue. He is tall and favors short-cropped hair, his missing tooth strangely giving him an even more appealing allure. Jamilu's nickname for me is "He Who Belongs to Loïza," my wife whose one-time visit in 1986 made a timeless impression. Jamilu would later go on pilgrimage to Mecca, where he remained for many years working his way up, as in Yekuwa, to ever greater financial heights. With the advent of satellite cellular service, he would begin telephoning me in Massachusetts on Sunday mornings from Saudi Arabia, just to hear my voice.

Our temporary departure from Yardaje causes as much commotion as do any of our other public appearances in the village. Today, our "appearance" is confined to taking leave of the chief and entering a vehicle.

"Do not leave anything behind," Schoolteacher Lawali cautions me. "There is no security once you have left."

"But we will be back in only a few days."

"It does not matter. Take everything." Our hut is indeed bare now, the only remaining trace of our passage being the flaps of cut fly netting that have been nailed into the two mud window frames.

My main preoccupation now is with the border crossing. The situation has greatly changed since I'd blithely passed from one country to the other on horseback: a Nigerian federal office now stands at the outskirts of the Yardaje marketplace, green-and-white flag fluttering above the misspelled "Boarder Station" signpost.

As our Land Rover stops we are approached by a civil servant in civilian dress. From his flatter facial features and Western-style clothing, I can see he is not from this northern part of Nigeria. It is also obvious that he is rather lonely in this rural frontier posting.

"We have guests and are bringing them home with us," the King of the Motorcars informs the customs agent in Hausa.

"Ah yes, I have heard about you," the fellow foreigner addresses me in schoolbook English. "You used to live in this village, isn't it?"

He does not ask my name or that of my son. He does not ask for passport or ID or departure stamp. Nor does he demand "What has been your mission in our country?" or "Why are you leaving Nigeria for Niger?" The forlorn customs agent merely inquires how long we will be gone and amiably wishes us a pleasant trip.

I have won the gamble! Or at least half of it. Although Sam and I are leaving the country, our visas for Nigeria have not been canceled. As long as we return across the boundary as informally as we have exited, we should have no problem at Immigration in the Kano airport.

But a few minutes after we've uneremoniously rolled across the invisible border ("That's it, Sam. We're in Niger!") the ambiance changes for the worse. Alongside the gravelly road, alone in the sandy savanna, stands a mournful shack and a grass hut: the *Poste de Douanes* (customs station) *de la République du Niger*. A steely soldier in khaki uniform stands several feet back, staring at the suspicious White Man and his boy in the Land Rover. He awaits the deferential walk that will bring him an explanation for this unusual arrival. In this contest of protocol, it is essential that Sam and I remain seated in the vehicle and feign absolute indifference to the officer.

My hosts' explanation of who we are, the account that had worked so well at the Nigerian customs post a few minutes before, impresses the Nigérien soldier not a whit. "They will need to see my superior," the *douanier* declares.

"Where is he?" asks Jamilu, King of the Motorcars.

"Probably in Sassambouroum."

It is the scenario I had imagined, in dread, long before we even left America. Not only would we be forced to make a long detour to the official immigration crossing—a scenario which my hosts had not anticipated when they obtained just a few bottles' worth of petrol for the short drive—but I might be interrogated about trying to enter Niger at an unauthorized crossing point. Worse, a particularly meticulous border guard might notice that Sam and I hadn't even officially exited Nigeria in the first place. Too many questions. Too many risks.

"Let's talk about this," King of the Motorcars suggests to the *soja* (soldier). He, the driver, the rest of our escort, and the soldier leave Sam and me alone in the Land Rover as they all retreat into the makeshift customs station. Sam and I experience our first shared moment of absolute Sahelian stillness.

Then, "What's going on, Dad?"

"Oh, nothing special. They're just taking care of formalities."

A few minutes later, full of smiles and thanks to the *soja*, our escorts clamber back into the Land Rover. But the ignition will not turn over. With nary a word, as if on cue, our hosts get back out and push start the vehicle. As we continue on our way. Jamilu, King of the Motorcars, emphatically denies my assumed regret that he must have had to fork over money to assuage the *douanier*.

"No, there was no 'nose eating,'" the King of the Motorcars assures me." Jamilu knows what I am thinking: to bring me home in style, in a vehicle, my friends have already borne the high expense of gasoline. Were there now the cost of an additional "dash"—a bribe—I would feel all the worse.

A few minutes later, just ahead of us, a figure in flowing robes, turban, and sunglasses—mounted but immobile on a motorcycle—waves furiously for us to stop. Afraid to chance another breakdown, we at first bypass the stranded biker. But then Jamilu recognizes him. "*Ku tsaye!* Stop! It's Alhaji Mallam Harouna!" We screech to a dusty halt. Alhaji Mallam Harouna, Muslim preacher, loyal friend, and horse correspondent, is uncharacteristically flustered as he dismounts from his two-wheeler.

"I'd wanted to meet you at the actual border line," he stutters, "but I had some troubles with the motorbike. No matter. I will tell you here and now what I wanted to tell you there, at the boundary. Come down from the Land Rover."

The air is still. Morning sun has already reached baking temperature. Sand glistens all around us. We are in the middle of the barren bush, alone except for the driver, escort, and my son. What is it that this Muslim priest, at whose nearby home we are supposed to stay, needs so urgently to say to us now? He takes my hands in his.

"Mista Bello, you and your son are welcome to Niger."

Only now do I realize what is happening. My friend had prepared a formal ceremony and speech for our boundary crossing. Here, in the middle of nowhere, he is delivering it.

"You have come in health, and in peace. We pray to Allah that, while among us, you and Samouel only continue to experience health and peace. It is our most sincere hope that, after your five days in Niger, when you return to Nigeria and re-embark for America, that you both feel a 'white heart' from your sojourn with us. Now, go back into the Land Rover."

No matter how many times in the past I had done it, arriving at Yekuwa after a couple of hours on horseback from Yardaje always made my heart skip a beat. From afar in the horizon—barely discernible from the silent, brown ocean of sand and bush—giant sugar bowl–shaped bins of woven millet stalks, hay, thatch, and rope emerge mirage-like on the outskirts of the village. These brown bins—*rumbuna*—contain the lifeblood of the village: the grains stored from one harvest season to the next. "Why is it that the storage bins ring Yekuwa," I'd once asked, "whereas those in Yardaje are hidden in the compounds of the village?"

"It's a matter of trust," came the answer. "In Yekuwa, no one will dare touch any other family's grain bin, so they can be out in the open. But in Yardaje, well . . . each family has got to keep an eye out on its own *rumbu*."

Beyond the *rumbuna* lay the grass houses which, in contrast to Yardaje's mud huts and corrugated roofs, make Yekuwa seem as if it literally grew out of the earth. Yekuwa thatch, rather than Yardaje adobe, similarly provides most of the compounds with a lighter tone of privacy. The spacious streets of Yekuwa—some of them broad enough to qualify as pedestrian boulevards—make Yardaje appear constricted in comparison. Enormous tree canopies sprout from open streets and compounds alike, providing much welcomed shade and an open invitation for townsmen to retire for conversation.

Depending on strength of steed and state of derrière, from first squinty-eyed glimpse of *rumbuna* to arrival at home hut in village center would take another twenty to thirty minutes on horseback. But now by Land Rover the entire trip, from Nigérien *douanes* to Yekuwa, whizzes by in barely quarter of an hour. How life has speeded up in my corner of Hausaland! The norm had been two hours by foot (somewhat less on horse or donkey); now, only villagers unwilling or unable to part with the equivalent of twenty cents travel the old way that, for me, had been emblematic of the Yardaje-Yekuwa lifeline. How easy life has become!

Hi! I'll give a little backup info. When I woke up this morning I had cold cereal (without milk) and tea. We then packed everything to go to Yekuwa. After saying goodbye, dodging & pulling away from the hands of children who didn't want me to go, we got in a large, old landrover. With our belongings, we set out to Yekuwa. We went through two custom stations, both causing no problems. We broke down a few times, but with a push-start, we were fine.

10

A delegation of Yekuwa elders in formal gowns and brimless hats await us: why is it that I am treated so formally, so respectfully, as if I were an official dignitary? The elders greet us and bless our stay. Despite the unpleasant sensation of not being able to recognize each face, or even to recognize the exact spot of this location in the village, I feel as if I have returned home.

When we arrived in Yekuwa we were engulfed not only by as many people as in Yardaje but 5 times more flies! In Yardaje, almost no one spoke English, but here in Yekuwa a lot of people speak French. So 2 points in favor of Yekuwa for communication.

Our baggage is unloaded at the home of Alhaji Mallam Harouna. We are ensconced in the heart of his compound, in the hut that he uses as his study for Islamic instruction. The hut is bursting with books and other religious paraphernalia; it is also well furnished, with mattress and tables. One of my lounge chairs from fourteen years before, now with just enough plastic strips to still constitute an actual seat, is retrieved. The cement wall surrounding our quarters is too smooth and high for even the most rambunctious kids to scale.

Still, these comfortable quarters constitute a logistical nightmare.

After we settled in a hut lent to us, all the people who had annoyingly been with us left. I took a shower in our unregular fashion (no details, please), went back to our room and (while dad snored) took a nap. I read a book most of the time before I remembered that I had to write.

The problem is this: our host's study is situated between the antechamber to his compound and his and his wives' sleeping quarters. In order to reach his own hut, he, his family, visitors, and students must all traverse the cement floor yard in front of our hut; likewise, to get to the street they must similarly parade in front of our temporary living quarters. However difficult it was to preserve a semblance of privacy for Sam in Yardaje, here in Yekuwa it will be absolutely impossible. I will either have to play doorman day and night or keep the doors continuously open, to legitimate comers and curious kids alike. Either way, Sam will not enjoy the exposure.

Beyond the psychological discomfort, I harbor a physical fear: bacterial infestation. Construction in cement, while a sign of wealth and modernity, encourages an insalubrious practice. Along the base of the compound walls, set in the cement ground, are sloping open gutters through which my host's neighbors evacuate their waste waters. There is no pumping mechanism, of course, and the slope is so gradual that much of the liquid waste stagnates before exiting our compound. Unlike in the house in Yardaje, and in most homes even in Yekuwa, there is no earthen or laterite yard space: the cement walls and floors, aggravated by putrid odors and the lack of privacy, incongruously convey the architectural ambiance of a prison block. Sam's concern is other:

"The Hole," the bathroom, is crawling with roaches. No wonder; it is not at all deep like in Yardaje, where you can drop something and count seconds until you hear thunk! *Euhew!*

As luck would have it, just as I come to greet Alhaji Aminu—the new chief of Yekuwa, in continuous palaver under a tree with other village elders—the rare rumble of a motor vehicle announces the arrival of another "guest": the newly posted gendarme responsible for Yekuwa's district. He is swaggeringly large, his belly protruding from his uniform and his beret a bit small on his skull. I sense nervousness in him as he surveys the bush village that for a year or two will constitute a big part of his beat.

We are uncomfortable in each other's presence: he knowing nothing about this White Man who has preceded him in the village; and I nervous about potential inquiries concerning our transborder entry into his turf. Neither of looks directly at, or even speaks to, the other: we are both Big Men, neither of whom can deign to make the first salutary move. Above all, my presence in this remote Nigérien village—even with the smaller, filial version of myself—must somehow come across as NORMAL. Normality demands that I treat this village as my own.

As the gendarme whizzes off, Land Rover wheels spinning in the sand, my own head spins about dubious border crossings, contested horse ownership, and imperative son protection.

Sam is not to remain Sama'ila for long. Apprised of the name change in Nigeria, our Muslim priest host decides to further Islamize my son's Hausa name. Henceforth, my son is to be known, at least in Niger, as Isma'il.

In Koran and Torah alike, Isma'il is no other than Ishmael, son of Ibra-him (aka Abraham, patriarch of the Hebrews). In English, the name is usually rendered as "God hears." The literal Hebrew root for "God" em-bedded in the name is El, a close-sounding cousin to Allah.

Ishmael, it should not be forgotten, was expelled into the desert with his mother Hagar by a jealous Sarah and a henpecked Abraham. But El-Allah took pity and sent an angel to rescue mother and child from the harsh wilderness.

And God was with the lad as he grew up,
he settled in the bush, and became an archer, a bowman . . .

fulfilling an even earlier divine prophesy: "he shall be a wild man of an ass."

Like his father, called Mallam Beel in Nigeria and Mista Bello in Niger, Samuel now has two names in Hausaland: Sama'ila and Isma'il.

Once a week in every village is market day. Every merchant goes to the town (or village) market and—sitting on mats in small, open huts (booths) for shade—sells his products . . .

It is certainly a risk, bringing Sam into the open market. For sure, un-less introduced to a Hausa market—its buzz of people, riot of colors, feast for the eyes—Sam will not have truly experienced Hausaland at all. But I can control the crowd here less than anywhere else. Within minutes we are surrounded by scads of kids pressing in on us, and become the main market attraction. I recreate a partial ambulatory cocoon, encircling my son with my two arms and sidestepping forward, crablike, from stall to stall.

At first I just walked around looking at stuff. I was content at the feeling that I could buy 2 of everything here and probably have money left over. I was going to buy oranges, but the merchant gave us 2 for free as a gift. Then we bought big gourds called "calabashes" and 5 féfés—calabash covers.

Faralu is with us, toting my bag and trying to prevent the kids from pushing and crowding us in. But he is not a person of great stature. De-spite his yelling and occasional lashes, we are completely surrounded.

We wandered a bit until I found a knife, about the size of my palm! I quickly bought it, and then I saw a pretty necklace. I bought 2, for my sister and mom. While I was buying these items (I was using my own money) dad borrowed some money and bought me a first-class, tricky-as-can-be, don't-look-at-me slingshot. Boy, does that thing shoot! At the next booth I bought a small mirror because (horror!) we had no way of properly combing or (in Dad's case) shaving.

Sam and I have basically triggered a small fan club riot, complete with dust storm kicked up by kids' feet. Despite the tumult I speak calmly to Samuel, reassuring him that he can inspect and buy anything in the market he desires. At the same time, the adults ceaselessly hail and greet us: "Mista Bello, Sannu da zuwa! Greetings on your arrival!" Virtually every merchant wants us to stop, chat, and shake hands. Only the mass of kids in the way prevents us from making hand contact with every stall keeper. I smile and return the greetings to the adults, feigning pleasure even as I contain a rising fear of claustrophobic panic for my son.

After a while I got bored of being followed and touched and petted. I asked if we could go home. But first I wanted some sugar cane. So off we went until I heard Dad say: "Oh, wow, Sam! Look at those!"

Occasionally, someone in the market yells out "Mallam Beel, Sannu!" I then know, because he didn't call me Mista Bello, that the greeter is visiting from over the border in Nigeria, very likely from Yardaje. And so I return the greeting with a joke: "Mi kake yi a nan? What are you doing here?"

There sat a knife seller. We wanted to buy his nicest knife, but the vendor indignantly refused, saying that that particular kind of knife was only for chiefs. So we got a different one (also beautiful) and then bought sugar cane.

My overwhelming preoccupation is securing space for Sam so that he can enjoy the market, buy a few items, and remember this as other than a riotous nightmare. But I also realize that the unruly mob risks alienating him from the heartbeat of Hausa life: the open marketplace.

At home, I realized the knife I bought was better because, besides being the only one with a sheath, it was sharper and stronger. I realized that when I used it to slice sugar cane.

Nighttime is the only opportunity to have serious, one-on-one, uninterrupted conversations: the daytime consists of one constant interruption, one series of greetings after another. I use the nights to conduct business, assured that Sam is secure in our hut and will not be disturbed.

At 9:00 pm dad told me to got to bed. I refused (though nicely) because I wasn't finished with my sugar cane. At 10:00 again he told me to go to bed. I grudgingly got ready for bed and brushed my teeth. By the time that was done, it was 11:00. So in the morning I was too tired to move.

During a quiet chat, I fully appreciate how faithful our host, Alhaji Mallam Harouna, is to his role as Islamic holy man. While fulfilling his perceived obligation to inform me from afar of my evolving horse problems, he will not now, even as I have traveled all this distance, condemn any of his fellow villagers. Nor will he intervene to apply the weight of his religious authority in my favor. He makes it clear, in a friendly but firm way, that the matter is for me to sort out, through the proper channels. For hospitality, for the safety of my son whom I leave alone in his charge, I can count on Mallam Harouna unconditionally. But with respect to intervening now in the horse problem, he observes a strict neutrality. We talk late into the night.

"You are really something," I tell my host, the Koranic scholar. "You have so much power in your pen."

"How is that?"

"Well, never once in your letters did you tell me I should return. All you did was to describe the situation. And yet the power of your words compelled me to take my son Isma'il and travel with him all this way—through Europe, through Nigeria, and now here."

"It is the power of God."

"Do you remember the conversation we once had," I continue, "the conversation about facing death?" He does not. Indeed, I am amazed that, for once, it is I, and not my Hausa interlocutor, who recalls a detailed exchange of many years past.

"I have often thought about it. The question was, 'If you are suddenly about to die—let's say in a traffic accident—would you like to know just before it happens?' You said no; I said yes."

"Why did you say yes?" Mallam Harouna asks, all inquisitive. After all, such existential questions are more his domain, as a holy man, than they are mine.

"I would like to prepare myself, even for my few final seconds." I go on. "To know that that's it: my life is over, that this is the conclusion to it. There is to be no more."

"And why did I say I wouldn't want to know?"

"For you, knowing the end of your life was at hand was too frightening. You didn't want to spend your final moments in fear."

"It is still true," the mallam reflects. Then he turns to me with a smile. He speaks, as always, in slow, measured tones.

"And do you remember when you accidentally locked Loïza in the hut?"

"What are you talking about?"

"You were about to go strolling and your mind was elsewhere. You forgot your wife was inside. So you locked the door, anyway." We laugh uproariously at my transcontinental absentmindedness. But I am also regretful: how many such incidents, grist for village lore, have I forgotten?

"Go to bed," my host suggests. "You are yawning."

"*Sai da safé,*" I say, ritualistically. "Until the morning."

"*Mun kwan lafiya,*" Alhaji Mallam Harouna responds. "May we sleep in peace."

"*Amin.*"

Crawling under the mosquito net in the Koranic preacher's study room late at night, I anticipate the early morning chill and wrap my sleeping son in the gray blanket I had procured six years before his conception. I drift off, still wondering: how much of my remembered life as Mallam Beel/Mista Bello has been overwhelmed by playing Professor Miles?

There is now stationed in Yekuwa a *hakimi*—a district-level chief. This is both a mark of importance for the village and a potentially disturbing development for Sam and me. Unlike the *mai-gari*, the village chief, who lives among the people and is easily approachable, a district-level chief acts as the august emissary of the *sarki*, the provincial chief, or king. Whereas the village chief administers, the district chief rules; if the *mai-gari* functions as the father of the community, the *hakimi* represents external authority. This particular *hakimi* is also the son of the Sarki of Magaria. How will this élitist take to Sam's and my unannounced arrival? Should I involve him in our horse troubles? Would he be a neutral party, or automatically rule in favor of his subjects against the stranger? At the very least we must pay homage, hoping he does not disturb the relationships I have cultivated for nearly fifteen years with the community and village chiefs.

On the outskirts of the village a huge, walled compound has been built for the *hakimi*. In the corner parallel to the antechamber, the robed royal holds court sitting in a chair under a large thatch overhang; huge mats, also in the shade of the thatch, are for prostrating and crouching courtesans and supplicants. In another corner is tethered a horse; in yet another, beyond a thatch fence, are the *hakimi*'s private quarters. A palace guard announces the arrival of visitors and we are ushered in to the compound. At seeing the large-hatted White Man and his smaller version sidekick, the *hakimi* struggles to contain his surprise.

"Bienvenu," he intones in French. "Welcome."

"Merci. Merci beaucoup. Nous sommes venus vous saluer. D'Amérique."

The *hakimi* enjoys showing off in front of his minions his ability to speak the White Man's tongue. Our skin color and language facility offset the subordinate position that sitting on the ground mat otherwise confers. English-speakers, white or black, do not command the same respect in Niger as do Francophones.

"Vous avez passé un bon voyage?"

"Oui, Dieu merci."

"Pas trop fatigués?

"Ça va."

"Et la santé?"

If it is incongruous to be speaking French with a Hausa chief in a Sahelian bush village, it is even stranger to be using Molière's language to exchange African idioms. All the customary greetings—inquiries into your health and that of your loved ones, your level of tiredness, your reaction to the cold season temperature—these are conducted according to Gallic rules of grammar and pronunciation.

We are a welcome diversion for the *hakimi*—especially after one of his retainers introduces himself as a former student of mine—and we are invited to return on the morrow. We will dine with the district chief.

We are honored. But how will I protect my son's stomach?

My wife, his mother, had warned me: "Take no chances with my son's diet!" Yet how can we reject a royal invitation? "Please understand," I begin our second visit saying to the *hakimi*, who has decked himself out in his ceremonial robes and, for Sam's sake, has even donned a sword, "my son is not used to African food."

"*Pas de problème*. Not to worry. I know all about that." We follow the *hakimi* to a shady spot near his living quarters, where he sits on one mat and Sam and I on another. With so many Hausa taboos relating to eating, it is a privilege just to see a high chief take lunch, much less feast with him. We are in an outdoor inner sanctum. Sam is beside himself, although he mixes up some of the chief's culinary explanations.

We had spaghetti (yum) and water from the well, and the most traditional West African food—something called boule (BOO-L) which is made of ox milk, millet & egg. Even with the big, big bag of sugar we put in, it tasted g-r-ooooo-ss.

For this one time I have neglected to bring bottled water with us, and Sam is exceedingly thirsty. Even the educated, Francophone *hakimi* prefers the brackish water of a nearby well to the crystal clear, pumped, water from the village center. Which is a greater risk for my son: dehydration or amoebic dysentery? Sam drinks brownish well water from the calabash.

The chief talked to dad about a ride on horses that will take place in the afternoon. I will ride the chief's horse, and Dad will ride on the town crier's.

Compared with what I have been scrounging together on our kerosene stove, this meal of pasta and gruel—shared with a high chief, no less—is a great treat. Yet at its conclusion, when Sam forgets his baseball cap on the straw mat, I again face frustration: while part of my brain remembers that there is a precise expression for "becoming forgetful or absentminded from the joy of eating," my memory fails to retrieve the Hausa word. Not long before, back in Yardaje, I'd had a similar experience when I jokingly tried to reproach Hassan for chatting while we ate together (Hausa decorum dictating that food be consumed wordlessly). Many years before this trip I had journeyed deep into Hausa culture to learn about such things as *santi* (full belly forgetfulness) and *gamsu* (frivolous dining chatter): now, with a blessed chance to demonstrate this knowledge, I suffer from a lack of vocabular recall.

It is like the dream I had back home just before embarking on this trip . . . I had just returned to Yardaje, and the chief was receiving me in his Bedouin tent out in the bush. (No such tent exists in reality but it is not hard—at least when asleep—to confuse the Sahel with the Negev.) I open my mouth to speak, but no Hausa words will come out: I have forgotten them all. Waves of sadness and frustration engulf me. It is the strain of trying to remember some Hausa words, and the actual, nocturnal effort of opening my mouth to utter them, that wakes me up.

When is it that it dawns on me? Here in Hausaland, I am absolutely immortal. Stuck in time, even. Everything that I do, that I have ever done—the length of local trips I once took, how much I spent eons ago for what purchase, whom I met where and what I then said—is etched in the memories and stories of the people around me. Even though I don't recall a fraction of these events past, they do. If a man's life is the sum of his experiences, then my Hausa acquaintances keep me more alive that I do myself. *Their* recollections of me in Hausaland are so much more accurate than my own. The villagers are more reliable witnesses to the life and times of Mallam Beel/Mista Bello than is Professor William Miles himself.

Dad's borrowed horse was dappled gray and mine black. Since my (faithful) steed was the chief of the region's horse, it was used to being in front. I didn't know where we were going so, with me pulling every which way to change directions, the horse got his share of discomfort.

The villagers' superior memories make me feel helpless. For by mastering my life and my deeds better than I do myself, in a sense the villagers control me. It is so sobering to realize that, long after my mind drifts back to my "regular" life, everything I do, say, give, or spend is recorded, forever, in the local collective consciousness.

From way up there (almost the clouds for me because I'm so short) the kids could still stare at but not touch me. They seemed to respect me for so skillfully maneuvering a horse, one of the most dignified animals in Africa. Sometimes we trotted but most of the time it was a fast walk. My horse (well, the chief's) was impatient and sometimes when I let it, it galloped.

Is my profile of anonymity in America as a "private intellectual," another obscure academic, aggravated or assuaged by being Mallam Beel/ Mista Bello in Hausaland?

Back at home, I wanted to get down by myself. A lot of people were ooing and aahing because for a short kid on a giant of a horse, it was a big jump. I knew how to do it because I had ridden ponies for a whole year in Mauritius. When I got down and went inside the house, though, my legs felt like jelly. That also happened when I rode a donkey in Israel.

This trip has awakened my dormant alter ego.

The horsy expedition was terrific.

To wake me up, my breakfast consisted of real tea with a serious amount of sugar ("Really, Sam!" Dad would say), matzah with honey, and raw cereal. We then went off to donate books and toys to the schools. There was 5th grade, 6thA, 6thB, 6thC, 7th, and 8th. Every time we entered a classroom, the students stood up. I wasn't surprised; that's what I had done with my class in a French school when I was in Mauritius. After all, Niger is a Francophone country.

Sam is doing me proud. In front of the elementary school principal, a teacher, and one of the classes, he agrees to read aloud the story chalked on the blackboard about a "little boy thinking about his pains and sufferings while working hard in the fields with his parents. They barely gathered enough money to buy bread. There was a talking sparrow who said, '*Il y en a avec moins que vous*: There are many with even less than you. Be happy with what you have.'"

He reads well, but not embarrassingly so, and slips on a word or two.

It is good for these little Nigériens see that, even for a white boy, it takes conscientious effort to read French.

When dad next visited the high school to donate books, I couldn't stand being touched and stared at anymore by the kids who followed. So I sat on the roots of a tree and read a book. I read & read and screamed at the kids not to stare at me, to go stare at and follow my dad instead, and to come out with what's so interesting about me.

Now when they stare at me, I close one eye and stare back. I like it when they realize I'm looking at them and they look away, embarrassed . . .

When we were walking home from the schools (here's another minor detail but Dad says all the details are important) there were grasshoppers everywhere, jumping further than I've seen in America. Neat!

We still need officially to announce our presence in Yekuwa! Jagga, the town crier, has the gestures of a court jester and the lungs of a bellow. And bellow he does, for a modest sum, going from corner to corner throughout the village to proclaim the news of our arrival.

Man, was that guy loud! Even from a distance his voice vibrated in me.

Jagga owns a horse these days (a white one—is it Sa'a's first replacement?), and I cannot resist the temptation. He will not only proclaim that my son Samuel is with me; Jagga will parade Sam from on high.

The town crier hoisted me up on his horse, with him sitting right in back of me. For 15 minutes and 41 seconds he yelled loudly in Hausa. It was deafening.

King Worker, He Who Belongs to Loïza, Announces:
'To the Town of Yekuwa—Morning Greetings and Greetings upon
    Arising in Health!'
The One Belonging to Loïza, He is Here in Yekuwa!

"Sam," I hastily translate, "did you hear? He's mentioning Mother." My son looks skeptical, even as Jagga continues blasting the proclamation throughout the village:

Menfolk and Women—Each and Everyone is Pleased!
Here He Is, in the House of Alhaji Mallam Harou and King Alhaji
    Aminu
To Reunite with All the People of Yekuwa, Kofai and Hamada!

Jagga is always diplomatic, reminding both sections of the village that, even if they were once split and still have separate chiefs, greetings for one entails greetings for the other.

Alhamdu lillahi! Praised Be to Allah!

Without lowering his volume a whit, Jagga addresses me:

You Who Belong to Loïza, You King Worker—How is Your Health?
You Have Slumbered, You Have Awakened
The Big Man of Yekuwa—Kofai and Hamada—Yardaje and
    Magaria!

Ah ha! So they are still aware of my sphere of influence . . .

We Thank You!

Is my own son as impressed with my prowess as this praise singer is?
Hard to tell . . . Wait—there is more:

"How Have You Slept?" bellows Jagga.
Sheepishly, I answer. "In health."

You've Slept Well? We Praise Allah!
Yekuwa—Kofai and Hamada—Look!
Here We are with Isma'ila, upon a Horse!
    Upon a Horse!
Jagga's Horse.

Is it embarrassment I see on my son's face? True, he is not used to
being lauded in such public fashion, but this is the highest form of Hausa
drama.

It Is Good!—Praise Be to Allah!
This is the Way I Like Things!

For a moment I can no longer follow what's happening. There is a question of money, and the phrase "naira to Jagga" pops out. Faralu turns to
me: "In your honor, this man"—he tells me the name—"has given Jagga
twenty naira." The praise singer is reinvigorated, and he turns again
to me.

You Have Slept, You Have Awakened!
Where Are You Going?
To Do the Work of a Governor!!
The Work of a Governor!!!

How easy promotion becomes in the mouth of a professional praise
singer! Jagga builds to the inevitable, if embarrassing, crescendo:

White Man!!!!!
The King Who Belongs to Loïza!!!
Lion!!!
Lion!!!
Lion!!!
Greetings!!!

Praised to high heaven in my borderline village, my son mounted—like a young prince—on a white horse with the town crier, I am flushed with pride. This is why I have traveled back into Hausaland with my progeny! This is what no other American father can claim to have achieved with his son!

I was mad at Dad. Even though I didn't want to go out of the house in the first place, he made me get on that horse with Jagga. Man, was he loud!

11

I ask to speak with Alhaji Aminu alone. The squat, round-faced, round-bellied chief in white robe takes me to his compound, the one he has inherited from his late uncle, Chief Danjuma.

Is this the same compound that I'd occupied over the course of an entire year? Where I'd installed an outdoor bed made out of date tree branches, sewn together with strips of goat hide leather? Where wobbly wooden chairs and tables enabled me to work, cook, and write upright outside, instead of crouching, as is the local practice, on the ground? Where I'd had a real door and windows with fly netting, plastic basins for washing, and a hay screen fence for private bathing?

None of these amenities is now present. Neither are the shelves, tables, chairs, and suitcases that had once filled the inside of the hut. It, too, is now empty, except for a single piece of Mecca-purpose luggage. My one-time luxury home in Hausaland has reverted to a simple adobe hut and courtyard, without a single frill in sight. Even a chief lives an ascetic life in rural Hausaland.

Chief Alhaji Aminu possesses a single chair, which he offers to me. But I am uncomfortable sitting above him, and request to get down and join him on the mat, "the way we used to do it."

"Yes, it is better," he agrees, shooing away the children who are already cramming into the compound.

"Or perhaps you should sit in the chair and I on mat," I banter, "since you have become chief."

"No, that's quite all right," Chief Alhaji Aminu chuckles.

Prelude is past; horse talk commences. It is the moment I have both long planned and feared. My rusty Hausa is now being put to the test, the greatest test to which I have ever subjected it since first arriving in Niger twenty-two and a half years before. This is not a matter of mere greetings or salutations, travel summaries or praise speeches. I need to reassert who I am. I need to resurrect Mista Bello.

I extend my right hand and, taking his, also grasp it with my left.

"Salaam Aleikum," says the chief. In a new sitting situation, we need to greet anew. "You are welcome. It is a pleasure to see you. How was your journey?"

"It passed in health."

"How is the mistress of the household?"

"Loïza asked me to greet you."

"Ah, thanks, thanks."

"And she said to greet the entire community."

"The entire community? We are thankful. We are thankful." He waits.

"Alhaji Aminu. I received word about the demise of the old chief."

"May he rest in peace," says the new chief in Arabic, a bolt of grief pocking his face and inflecting his voice.

"May Allah rest his soul," I commiserate in Hausa. "May Allah preserve us all. May Allah allow the old chief to rest in peace."

"Amen."

"This is the first thing I wanted to say."

"There is no fault in it."

"I remember him. Just like before, when I used to live here as a son of the village.

"It is so."

"That is the reason I have come. With Sama'ila. Together with him."

"We are thankful."

I pause.

"Too much time has passed since I last left. But I have not forgotten the people."

"The people," Alhaji Aminu repeated. And then he invokes a word I'd forgotten: *masoya*.

"*Masoya*?"

"Those whom one loves. Those with whom you have a strong relationship. Those who are close to you there, in your heart."

"Although Hausa comes to me with difficulty nowadays, I still retain all the trust, the remembrance, and the friendship—all of it," I respond.

"May it be Allah's will. Praise be to God."

"This is why I have come. So that I see you, and so that you see me. As in times past."

"Yes, it is proper," Alhaji Aminu chimes in.

"You haven't forgotten me, I haven't forgotten you."

"Allah is great! Always, we are thinking of you. Always. When word came that Mista Bello was returning, when we received your letter, everyone was happy. Everywhere I went, people asked me to greet you. Everybody."

"I am pleased."

"Praise be to Allah." Chief Alhaji Aminu pauses for me to continue. I do so, using a formal expression to denote a change of subject.

"Moreover, this time I have not come alone."

"Yes."

"I have come with my son."

"May he too be in health."

"Sama'ila. My heir."

"It is so."

"Because he has begun to understand the ways of the world."

"You need to show him everything. How you lived among us. The bonds. And all the things you left behind—what has become of them."

"Yes, precisely!" Now that the chief has opened the critical topic, I am hoping he will continue. But he doesn't. So I retreat toward more familiar terrain.

"We have come so that he sees you all. And so that all of you see him."

The chief does not respond.

"So that he sees all the people in Yekuwa. All the people I've told him about."

"Hmm."

"So that he sees and knows every little thing for himself, including all the friendships. Everything."

"Hmm." The chief waits for me to proceed.

"Moreover . . ."

"Proceed."

". . . we need to discuss the matter of inheritance."

"Ah ha!"

"Because if Allah takes me away—if I die—that is what I leave behind."

How legalistic the word "inheritance" sounds in English! Does it not conjure up lawyers, wills, estate taxes, and other unpleasant formalities? Houses to sell, money to divide, proceeds from probate? It is such an ambivalent concept—a welcome windfall of wealth sullied by its inevitable association with the death of a loved one.

In Hausa, though, the equivalent concept—*gado*—conveys so much more than material benefit. Embodied in the word is the spirit of the departed, so that you inherit not merely the deceased's objects but his soulful legacy. "Patrimony"—the historical heritage of a family, people, or nation—would be a more accurate translation, but is not a term used in normal discourse. When the chief and I speak of "inheritance," then, it means much more than the imparted possessions of the dead: we are talking about the future, about preserving the memory, the very soul, of the original owner.

We do not shun discussing death in Hausaland. It is a common reality well integrated into community life. Death—including our own—is not the taboo subject it usually is in polite discourse in the West.

"Isn't it so?" I ask. "If God calls me, do I not pass on my *gado*?"

The chief falls silent. He is not willing to broach the horse problem himself. I try another tack.

"Before, we had a patriarch in my family. His name was Samuel. He was my father, but he passed away before I ever came here. Look, here he is." Chief Alhaji Aminu looks intently at my photo album. "We gave his name to my son."

"*Allah Akabar*. This way, you are always reminded of your father. *Allah Akabar*: God is great. This is good, what you have done."

"It is our custom. This is what we do to preserve the past, to keep our traditions."

"It is our custom, too, so that we too remember the patriarchs of our families as well. After the old chief died, we gave his name to the next newborn. It's the same thing." He stops.

Again, Chief Alhaji Aminu forces me through silence to take the conversational lead. I can circumvent no more. My speech slows, as my brain scans frantically to recover the necessary, precise Hausa vocabulary.

"All right. Regarding the inheritance—it too is a matter of trust, about which I spoke to you earlier. A sign. Of trust. That I left in the hands of the chief."

"You speak of the former chief? The one who passed away?"

"Yes, the one who passed away—May Allah rest his soul."

"Amen."

"In trust, I left this sign. Not as a matter of money. As a matter of trust. And of friendship."

"For these reasons you left him something."

"Yes. But there was not only the symbol that you saw. There was also a document."

Carefully, I unfold the written agreement and, grasping it with both hands, hand him the paper. Chief Alhaji Aminu takes it, also with both hands. "This is the agreement that he put his hand to, concerning 'the sign of trust.' That is, concerning the . . ." I force myself, at last, to utter the word: the word that, on account of discretion, diplomacy, and *kumya*— the Hausa sense of shame—I have avoided all along. ". . . *doki*. The horse. The one I left in his hands."

"Allah is great."

"See the signature of the old chief." Unsure of Chief Alhaji Aminu's level of literacy, I point to the spot.

"Ah hah."

"It's not a 'copie,'" I explain, borrowing one of the few French words that has made its way into Nigérien Hausa. I tap the paper, as if to demonstrate its authenticity. Then I borrow an English word that is in common use in Nigerian Hausa. "It's an 'original.'"

"An 'original,' the chief repeats, nodding. "I understand."

"For fourteen years," I continue, "I have held on to this paper, in my very abode. Look here, the signature of the Galadima,"

"Yes, it is here, the signature of the chief's main adviser." We agree that the signature of Faralu, my horse groom, is also on the paper.

"Well . . . ," I offer, hoping the chief will pick up the thread. But he still doesn't bite. "Proceed," he murmurs.

"I thought—I believed—that whenever I returned, I'd find my horse."

"Hmm."

"But now I understand that I cannot mount my horse. I cannot canter, I cannot gallop. I cannot do everything that I used to. The reason I left the horse in the first place was so that whenever I returned I could do all these things again. Or so that, even if I didn't return, my heir could still come, claim it, and . . ."

The chief broke in. "So that even Sama'ila, could come and ask, 'Where is it?'"

"This is why I have come to you."

"Hmm."

"So that we discuss this horse inheritance. And do what you deem necessary."

"Ah hah!"

"I do not feel anger."

"No," he reassures me, "there is no need to worry . . ."

"Nor," I insist on continuing, "is it a matter of money. The money that I spent in coming here . . ."

The chief interrupts. ". . . is certainly more than the value of the horse. We know that. Traveling on an airplane is very costly."

"So I have come to your abode to hear what you have to say."

"About?"

"About the horse inheritance."

"Horse talk." His tone seems to say, So the time to discuss the horse business has finally come.

"Yes. So that we resolve the problem completely, keeping in mind my heir."

"You have spoken truthfully."

"Is this not the way it should be?"

"Yes, this is the way it should be."

Yet I still have to express apologies, on two accounts. First, "a guest am I, a visitor. I came to your community and lived as a 'son of the village'. . ."

". . . in trust."

". . . yes, in trust. But on account of me there has been fighting, a coming to blows, and . . ." I intend to use the term for "trouble, agitation, anger"—*tashin hankali*—but instead mistakenly say *rishin hankali*— "foolishness."

"Don't let your soul be disturbed on account of it."

"My soul *is* disturbed on account of it. So I apologize, if because of me there has been all this uproar, this tumult."

"Hmm."

"And I also apologize because my Hausa is not what it used to be. It's finished, worn out." This is stronger than what I mean—"broken, rusty" is what I want to say (*'bace*, not *kare*)—but the chief lets my adjective pass without correction. Maybe my language facility is a lot worse than I'd feared.

"All right." The chief changes his tone. At last, he will discourse.

"This is what we know—are you following? In actual fact, someone has trampled on your path toward the inheritance. Naturally, no one wanted to hurt or to do wrong. To the contrary, there was always the question: 'What if the European returns and asks for his inheritance? Where is the trust then?' So we called a big meeting about it, and everyone came to listen."

Alhaji Aminu speaks in his signature raspy, high-pitched voice. Several words are swallowed in an upper-level register. Since Hausa is a tonal language to begin with, it is an especial strain to disaggregate his speech.

"There was a gathering of the people and a thorough recounting of the facts, just as you have given. 'This horse did not belong to the late chief but to Mista Bello. Everyone knows this. Here are the signatures.' Galadima spoke and so did Faralu. Everyone looked at the chief's own signature.

"But for the survivors of the chief, the offspring that he left behind, they saw things differently. To their eyes, the horse belonged to their father. We gathered all of the chief's immediate family, all of them, and we told them otherwise.

"'It is his, even if he decides to go galloping with it in America. For ten years we took care of his horse. In health. We rode it, we groomed it, and everyone knew that he had entrusted it to us. Allah forbid that anyone say otherwise.'

"Eventually, we saw that this horse was growing old. It was time to replace it: we sold it, and bought another."

"There is no blame," I say, in absolution. How can I hope to recover a horse that has been gone for four years already? Let title be transferred from Sa'a to his successor. "Sam will have to understand."

"Fine. There was this new horse, we lived next to it. You could have seen it, had you come: the one you would actually be leaving as an inheritance. We even wondered 'What if we use up all the days that Allah has allotted us?' All kinds of things we talked about, as is our wont, so that the day never comes when you and we be completely separated.

"And we even wondered about the day that you would pass on your *gado*, your inheritance. 'Mista Bello is gone, he has left this world far behind!' Then one day your heir would come, if he is alive and healthy. It would not be for our little ones to inherit the horse but your heir.

"We prayed to Allah that, just as we grew close to you, so should our heirs grow close to your children, and to your grandchildren. Including," chuckles the chief (before adding the precautionary "May Allah leave him alone"), "the House of Isma'ila!" Then, suddenly, in deadly seriousness, the chief intones:

"The confiscation of your horse is against God's law. Do you want me to summon the one who . . . ?"

I am trapped in confusion. I do not know whom the chief is talking about, or why I should demand to see this person. Until now, I had assumed that the chief himself had been in some way implicated in the horse snatching. Now he is asking my permission to take another—but whom?—to task.

It is exactly the kind of panicked haze that I had feared I would encounter, the result of incomplete comprehension or outright miscomprehension. It is as if I am in tenth grade chemistry again, being interrogated at the blackboard by a tyrannical science teacher who assumes I can decipher and recalculate the chemical equations in front of me. It is not complete gibberish to me, but I am still missing a few mental links to make it click all together . . .

". . . Shall we summon him to 'pour out' this same talk upon him, and to show him your paper?"

The chief now spoke more tentatively. "We'd tell him, 'Are you still trying to forget the matter? We have not forgotten. The original paper has caught up with you. Plus, I have already spoken about this, with my own mouth. You didn't care.' I'll be able to say that there is now speech greater than my own.

"I'll say, 'Mista Bello has come to me for judgment, for I am chief.' As for his brothers . . . I'll tell him that he needs to speak to them himself.

I now realize that Alhaji Aminu is not declaiming; he is thinking out loud. The chief is articulating a strategy, formulating reasons for what he will say to the summoned man. Much of his musings out loud escapes me. I do not understand why he has not done all of this before, why he did not see to it that my indisputable claim was not respected all along. If the chief of Yekuwa had been upholding my horse title from the beginning, why had my son and I needed to leave America for Africa in the first place? This mental fog, aggravated by my rusty Hausa, is agonizing.

"*A kira shi?*" the chief asks me, several times over.

"*A kira shi,*" I hear myself say. "Summon him."

12

When dad came home from the village chief's office, we took bottles filled with water and soap and washed. It was refreshing, especially because it was the hottest part of the day—over 40 degrees Andrew Celsius and 100 degrees Fahrenheit! Ouch! We always rest after taking baths because the heat makes people drowsy. I read a book, dad slept, and I started writing. It took me a while to realize that someone was knocking at the door. I hurried to open it. As I was walking (or running) to the door, a reception of lizards scattered. One ran over my foot, which wasn't pleasant. I was freaked for a second. Then I laughed and, after opening the door, chased and caught a few lizards. I looked one in the face and as it flicked its tongue out to taste the air, I pretended to be offended and stuck my tongue out at him too.

Sitting before me now, still in the chief's compound, is a man I do not recall ever having seen before. He is leaner than the chief, a bit taller, and more muscular. His voice is also the opposite of Chief Alhaji Aminu's: bass, loud, brusque. Even as he unstintingly utters the formal pleasantries, I viscerally sense an inauthenticity in his speech.

What is his name? What is his relationship with the chief? Who was he to the late chief? These are key matters, but events have been moving so rapidly that I haven't had the time or opportunity to sort them out. To ask such basic questions at this point would be unseemly, embarrassing. It is assumed that I know and remember so much that I do not. Nor do I yet know that my host Alhaji Mallam Harouna had, exactly thirteen months prior, written a memorandum to himself documenting in detail the origins of the horse dispute. Sharing the memo's contents with me earlier would have spared me my current confusion and uncertainty. Perhaps like a Zen master, my priestly host wants me to work through and discover the truth myself. This is what Alhaji Mallam Harouna wrote in Arabic-scripted Hausa:

> In the Islamic month of Shawal, on the fifteenth day, on a Tuesday, Alhaji Amadou Jaki took the chief's horse, the one that Mista Bello—

the White Man in America—had left in trust. He took it to the market in Garke and sold it for seven thousand naira.

Alhaji Mallam Ibrahim, Oumarou, and Habibu—they're the ones behind it.

I, Alhaji Mallam Harouna, upon hearing that this illicit act was about to transpire, informed the *hakimi* so that he instruct the men not to do this. But they ignored the *hakimi* and sold the horse.

Before me is Brah—nickname for Ibrahim—the ringleader. So *he* is our chief antagonist! It is he who claimed the horse for himself and his brothers, rejecting all reminders of the beast's original ownership. It is he who had the horse wrested away, brought to market, and sold. It is he sitting before me in Chief Alhaji Aminu's compound, speaking quickly in a harsh, guttural, voice. The chief and Faralu, my former groom, are the only other adults present. As usual, we are also hemmed in by crowding children and buzzing flies.

"Have you come in health?" asks my nemesis.

"In health."

"How has life been?"

"In health."

"Greetings."

"You know this man, don't you?" Chief Alhaji Aminu asks me.

"Yes, I know him."

"Only his name you have forgotten. It's Mallah Brah."

"Oh, yes," I kid. I try a joke. "Only he's aged." Alhaji Aminu and Faralu laugh.

"It's on account of our household," Brah replies firmly, seriously. "On account of all the worrying, since the old chief died. That is what has brought about this change."

I extract from my leather bag the enlarged, black-and-white print of the late chief that I had shown Chief Alhaji Aminu at our earlier pow-wow. Aminu had been visibly shaken by the sight of it, undoubtedly the only image of the departed Danjuma in existence. When I'd told the chief I would be leaving the print as a gift, he expressed much gratitude. When I show it now to Brah, he too is visibly moved.

"I am leaving it for the chief's heirs," I announce stupidly. Chief Alhaji Aminu gives me a look. Hadn't I said I'd be leaving it with him?

I have committed yet another gaffe. In my mind, all these surviving relatives of the late chief are, in some communal sense, his heirs. It is a naïve thought, as naïve as the advice of all my friends back home in America that "the village" ought to sort out my horse mess; or that I should donate the horse to "the village." But there is no single "village mind" or "village will." Why do we expect a unanimity within African communities that we are far from possessing in our own?

"Let the chief protect and preserve the photo," I declare, with a trace of indecision.

"*Madalla*" responds Chief Alhaji Aminu enthusiastically. "Thank you."

"*Madalla*," repeats Mallam Ibrah, less enthusiastically.

"May Allah preserve the soul of the old chief," I pipe in, flustered. "That is the first of three items I wish to discuss."

As Chief Alhaji Aminu puts the picture away Mallam Ibrah comments. "Take good care of it. It is something to make one weep."

There is a long pause. Chief Alhaji Aminu, as is his wont, places the speaking burden on me. "Now your second item of discussion," he prompts me.

"Right. The second item," I say, looking at Brah, "is this: I have not come alone."

"Fine."

"Maybe you've seen him, maybe you haven't, but I've come with my son."

"I've seen him. We greeted each other. I spoke to him."

"That boy is my heir."

"Uh huh."

"That is the one whom Loïza gave birth to."

"Yes."

"He bears the name of our *babban gida*—the founder of our household—the name of my very father."

"Your old man."

"After me follows Isma'il."

"It is good."

"Moreover, I wanted to bring him here because I have grown accustomed to the people. And the people have gotten used to me. We have established friendship, and trust."

"For sure."

"I have lived in this very compound, the home of the old chief. I have lived here!"

"Allah is great," the chief chimes in.

"Moreover, in my plans to return, there was something—a horse . . ."

"Yes . . ."

". . . that I entrusted to the chief."

"Uh huh."

"For a horse is something I take great pleasure in having. Riding, can-tering, galloping—touring the countryside on horseback, so that I can see the people and they can see me."

"May it be Allah's will."

"That is the reason I did not wish to sell it."

"Yes."

"For me, riding a horse is more precious than its value in money. And I told myself, 'One day, if it pleases Allah, I shall return. Maybe it will take five years, or ten—but no matter how long it takes, I will have my horse. I've gone through much trouble buying horses, going to the markets of Maiaduwa, of Garke—buying, selling, buying, selling. To avoid all this trouble I prefer leaving my horse here. Whenever I return, I'll just mount it and ride. After that, I'll leave it with the chief, so that he too can make good use of it. If Allah should take me away and I am no longer alive, after me there is my heir. He knows that we have a horse here in Yekuwa. He too will come and ride.' Well, here we are. We have returned."

"Allah has brought you safely."

"The old chief is no more, may Allah rest his soul."

"Amen."

"And there is no horse."

"Hmm."

Silence.

"The amazing thing," I say, hoping Brah will finally step up to the plate, "is that the 'sign of trust'—the horse—is not here. Here is the document that the late chief put his hand to. Shall I read it?"

"Read it," Chief Alhaji Aminu says. After the recitation, I point to the name of each witness and conclude, "Here is your father's signature." Silence.

"It is not a matter of anger," I declare, solemnly, folding the paper.

"No anger," Brah repeats. Then, finally, he speaks, but in such a rapid-fire Hausa that even my tape recording offers little clarification: da-ta-da-ta-da-ta-da-ta. But I catch the drift.

"You see, Mista Bello, something happened to our copy of that paper that you just showed. That's why there was a problem. We sold the horse, it's true. But when we sold it, we said, 'When Mista Bello comes back, we'll return to him all the money we got for the horse.' So now you have come. There is no need for scandal. We'll retrieve the money and give it to you. *Ranke ya da'de*."

This last sentence sets me aback. All along I have been bending over backwards to settle this problem man-to-man, from one "son of the village" to another; I have not, for instance, weighed in with the *hakimi* or gone to an *alkali*, a Muslim court judge. Yet here the horse snatcher invokes a phrase reserved to demonstrate humility before royalty and powerful government authorities.

"It's not the money I'm after," I try to make Brah understand. I want to explain, even to the man who masterminded the hostile horse take-over—*especially* to the mastermind of the takeover—that I am yearning, above all, for affirmation of the trust that I'd placed, through his father, in the entire community. I want him to see the horse as I do, as sign of an ongoing bond with all of Hausaland. I need Brah, Aminu, Harouna—everyone—to know that, tied up with horse title in Yekuwa, are my and my son's deepest feelings of attachment to all of Africa.

But I can say none of this adequately. Not in Hausa. Perhaps not in any language.

"You've spoken with the chief, haven't you?" Brah continues in his high-speed Hausa. "You know that we didn't just sell your horse and replace it once, right? First we bought a white one. Then we sold that one, and bought another one, a black one. That was the one the chief had when he died.

"But the money we got for the horse is still around. We'll gather it all together and return it to you."

Could it really be so simple? Have my ten-year-old son and I really needed to travel from suburban America to remote Niger via Holland and Nigeria—taking one airport bus, two KLM flights, one chauffeured minivan, and a rusting Land Rover—just to have this simple five-minute chat guaranteeing a horse refund?

"You're here tomorrow, aren't you?" Brah wants to know. "How about the day after?"

In truth, we have four days left before commencing our return journey. Yet I am reluctant to tell him so, lest Brah use this logistical knowledge against us: I remember too well having been singed in my first Hausa horse sale twenty-one years before. Still, I tell him accurately, "There are four days remaining."

"Four days, huh? All right." Brah continues, his words spewing from his mouth in Hamito-Semitic staccato. "Before those four days are up we will bring you the money that we got from selling it: six thousand naira." Six?

There are looks all around. Then he admits, "That's less the three hundred pounds"—colonial British currency terms are still used in current calculations—"that we gave to the one we sent to the market to make the actual sale. Then there was the commission for the King of the Horse Sellers, and the witness money . . ." As Brah itemizes and deducts eight hundred worth of "incidental costs" from his offer, I decide not to quibble over a single one.

"If Allah wills it," Brah concludes, employing one of countless conditional idioms that recognize Muslim man's subordination to divine will, "before you leave, you will have all your money back. If Allah wills that we cannot gather all of it before your departure, then we'll give you half of it right away. But the actual horse—the third one—you've got to understand that it's been sold."

"I understand," I commiserate. "There is no blame in your talk."

"Uh huh! You see, Mista Bello, this matter has become a matter of what we call here in Daura *tsegumi*—scandal." Yekuwa, I can't help recalling, had in fact been severed from the kingdom of Daura nearly a century before, during the colonial carving up of Hausaland into Nigeria and Niger. But this is no moment to digress on local history and politics. Stick to the horse business, Mista Bello!

"We want to erase this blemish, this stain. This is our home. We live here. Everything is in God's hands. May Allah grant you patience in this matter, patience with me and with my brothers."

Conflicted feelings, complicated thoughts. Yes, I have achieved victory—my claim to the old chief's horse is vindicated through the promise of monetary restitution. But if anyone believes that I am satisfied with a mere refund of horse money, then I have lost. I take time to formulate my words, struggling to speak at a level of Hausa that is fifteen years behind me:

"This money you're offering: I can't mount it. I can't canter with it. I can't gallop with it . . ."

Brah interrupts with a dismissive laugh. "How much did you pay for your original horse? Now look how much you're getting back in return. We're not offering the six hundred naira you paid for horse number one. Six thousand naira we're prepared to give."

The intensity of his retort and the strength of his logic overwhelm and silence me. Eventually, Chief Alhaji Aminu chirps in.

"Well, Mista Bello. You've heard what Brah has had to say. We are awaiting your answer." I will not, however, be rushed into speaking.

"I still prefer," I finally—and stubbornly—maintain, "a 'sign of trust'— a horse. If there is still money from the horse sale, then let another one be bought. But I want my heir to see his horse."

Brah bursts into happy Hausa. He *hears* that I have accepted his proposed resolution. He does not understand my actual demand: that he and his brothers take on the responsibility of procuring a new *doki*, and that they do so before Sam and I leave. But this is not the way that things are done in Hausaland . . .

"Mista Bello," Brah rumbles in his quick, gruff voice, rising from his mat, "it's time for mid-day prayers. Let us go to the mosque and pray. Think about what we have said. We will hear your response this afternoon."

There is something I still need to say. "I have not come to squeeze you," I tell him feebly, in a final attempt to efface the shame of a bleeding-heart liberal shaking down a miserable African villager and his unfortunate brothers. But how can poor Brah ever comprehend what a dumb horse means for this crazy White Man?

As we leave Chief Alhaji Aminu's compound, and I muse ambivalently about how easy the showdown has actually turned out to be, Faralu stops at the side of the thatched compound fence and rebukes me: "Why did you tell him that you don't mean to squeeze him? He's going to find a way out of it now. You heard what he said: he'll give you the horse money if Allah wills it. And maybe not even all of it." He shakes his head in disgust.

Deep down, I know that Faralu is right. I'd been had in horse matters before. Unless I am extremely careful, I am likely to be taken again for a ride. Despite his words, I did sense an insincerity in Brah's tone that I cannot, despite his repeated reassurances, easily dismiss.

How far am I to take this game? How hard am I to push for the money, now that I have extracted unequivocal vindication by my nemesis? And what would I do with more gigantic bundles of naira even in the unlikely event that they appear? Give them to my son, my heir? Give them to the horseless groom, turning him into a veritable instant millionaire?

I ask Faralu for advice. Faralu, my erstwhile "boy," the new chief's gofer.

Faralu, who owns maybe two shirts and a single pair of pants. Faralu, the diminutive, plain-speaking brunt of many a village joke. My simple, increasingly toothless, guileless Faralu. "But if Brah actually turns up with the money," I ask him, "wouldn't you want it? Or would you actually prefer me to buy another horse?"

Until this moment I have been taking Faralu for granted—much as I probably did in sojourns past. Yet it is his response that allows me to fully understand why I have needed to return to Yekuwa. It really has not been on account of the horse at all.

"Do you hear me, Mista Bello?" Faralu always spoke loudly to me, as if I were the slow one whose comprehension would be enhanced by greater volume. "Do you hear? If it were up to me, you would buy another horse."

"Why? Wouldn't you want the money?"

"Don't you see? All those years that you weren't here, I took care of your horse. Whenever I rode it, even deep in the bush, people would recognize me and shout, 'Look at Faralu on Mista Bello's horse!'

"But when the dispute arose, and the horse was gone, some people were saying: 'It was a lie. The horse didn't belong to Mista Bello after all this. Faralu made it all up.'

"That's why I want you to have the horse replaced, so that I can take care of it once again. Only that will prove to everyone that I was in the right all along."

Faralu's words trigger an epiphany. All these years it has been he, more than anyone else, who has, day in and day out, preserved my memory and "sign of trust" in Hausaland. By feeding, watering, exercising, and grooming my horse—two incarnations of which I'd never even set eyes on—it is he who has kept alive, in affection and with loyalty, the living symbol of my presence in this corner of the Nigerian-Nigérien borderlands. It is he who exchanged bitter words with Brah in public, defending me thousands of miles away; it is he who was physically roughed up shortly before my horse was rustled away.

Faithful Faralu, to whom I am ashamed to admit I had given little thought all these years: it is for his sake, even more than my son's, that I need to resolve my African horse problem. It is his honor, his face, his reputation that is most at stake. It is Faralu—who doesn't even possess a last name—whom I ought to defend. But am I really prepared to "squeeze" Brah and his brothers to do so?

On the way back from greeting the chief of the other Yekuwa (and giving him a green carpet as a gift) we were accompanied once more by the kids, creating so much dust that I sneezed more times than I have cells in my body.

I am torn between two selves: the American me, desirous not to stoke any unnecessary fires even as I breeze in to spin an exotic yarn for my son and posterity; and the Hausa me, not above but of this village, with allies, obligations, and inescapable partisanship.

When we arrived home (and got rid of the children) Alhaji Mallam Harouna came and told us he had gone to another village for market day and had bought some things for me—two slingshots (with frilled rubber strands), two big pieces of sugar cane (one of which I have eaten already) and 4 oranges.

Now I'm on the mat outside the hut writing, thanks to the flashlight aimed by a French-speaking man. I'm about to have some couscous with tomatoes. Mashed tomatoes, now. Yuck!

Dad has asked me what I think we should do about the horse money: keep it or use it to buy a new horse? I'd rather have an orange. (Just kidding!)

13

Although he will not pass judgment or provide direct advice, our scholarly host, Alhaji Mallam Harouna, is an excellent sounding board. The afternoon has slipped by and I still have not conveyed my decision to the chief and to Brah. Yet what decision is there to make? On what grounds can I refuse the six thousand naira offer, even if I (and Faralu) are skeptical of Brah and his brothers actually getting the money together before Sam's and my departure? We have come for an inheritance horse, not for monetary compensation. I am mulling things over with my host when, out of the darkness from the compound antechambers, a figure appears:

"*Asalam aleikum*," he calls out, using the Arabic greeting which I still automatically, Hebraically, translate as *Shalom aleichem*. "Peace unto you."

He comes in carrying a paper, the type ripped out of French school notebooks. "Alhaji Mallam Harouna, a message for you."

My friend slowly unfolds the paper as I bow my head to illuminate: every day at dusk I affix a miner's type flashlight to my forehead, freeing my hands for the evening and assuring I never forget where I've left the lamp. Looking at the paper I am reminded of how it feels to be illiterate: the message is written in *ajami*, Hausa words in Arabic script. For me it is Yiddish-in-reverse: Germanic words in Hebrew letters.

Alhaji Mallam Harouna furrows his brow, before forcing a smile. "It's from Brah," he says, shaking his head. My host, my friend, is reluctant to convey the contents.

"Please read it," I ask.

"*Wasiksa daga hannun Mallam Ibra Bira*," he deciphers, conveying the traditional Hausa letter writing form. "A letter from the hand of" my nemesis. "To Mallam Harouna, Son of a Jackass."

This cannot be right. Once again, my rusty Hausa must be failing me. Could Brah have sent my host such a brazen insult in writing, under his own name and during my very stay?

"You have brought Mista Bello to Ibrah Bira," Alhaji Mallam Harouna continues reading. "All that remains is that you bring forth the Angel of Death."

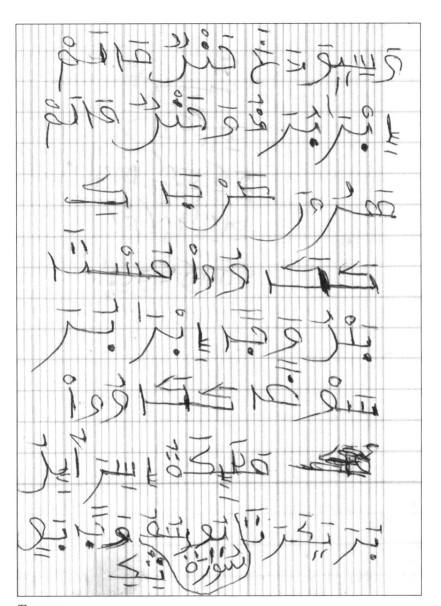

The curse.

What have I wrought? Has my quest to restore justice and honor in the form of a horse degenerated into death threats against my defenders? Against me? Have I put my son at risk?

"We are used to him being like this," my host reassures me when he sees me seething. "He has a hard head. For us, it's nothing new that he uses such language." Mallam Harouna continues. "You ought to be patient and forbearing with him." But I cannot. This threat is my tipping point. With it disappears the last shred of Bature objectivity I'd been harboring, the paternalistic attitude of viewing the horse dispute coolly and from some antiquated anthropological distance.

From this moment forward I am, once again, *completely* Mista Bello, ready to use every arm at my disposal to protect my interests and the people here who are on my side. Who is this Brah to threaten Mista Bello's selfless host!?!

Despite the late hour, I ask Alhaji Mallam Harouna to bring me to the chief immediately. We leave Sam in the hut, with several trusted friends in the courtyard to watch over him.

Even at this late hour, the chief is out. Mallam Harouna and I wait. In Hausaland, this is an art one needs to cultivate: the art of waiting.

Dad went to the chief's house to talk about the horse. I was at home, and after a while I got bored. A French man [a villager who speaks French] showed me the exit to the compound so that I could find Dad in the village labyrinth. I wandered until I found the French man again. He was taking a walk, too, I guess. He asked a few people around a fire if Dad had been passing around there. The French man (who, like everyone, also spoke Hausa) translated: "At the chief's house." I wandered in the direction they pointed in, heard Dad's voice, and entered the compound. Was he surprised to see me—he thought I was at home!

Even with a full moon, I am amazed that Sam can navigate his way through the village at night. Straw huts and fences cast strange shadows on the sandy streets. It is still; it is very late. We have a rare opportunity: to stroll through the village alone, without a swarm of overenthused children, without continuous hailing and greeting and crowding. It is a pity that Sam can only appreciate the physical beauty of Yekuwa at night.

The chief wasn't home, though. He was at the police station because there had been a dispute about a bull. So we decided to take a walk around the village: We did, and met a lot of people who were in groups, laying around a fire.

From afar, from America, most people dismiss my legal problem in Hausaland as quaint or comical merely because it's over a horse. But what if the illicitly transferred item were not a horse but a stock certificate? What if the dispute were not over a quadruped but a bank account? What if we were talking about a purloined municipal bond instead of a heisted herbivore? Why would that make people back home view the matter more seriously?

On our way home, we saw the chief coming back. So we returned to his compound and Dad spoke with him, while I almost fell asleep on the mat.

The "evil words" of Brah do not perturb Alhaji Aminu: he takes both insult and threat in stride. "This is his temperament," the chief informs me. "We're used to it." When he sees that I do not share his equanimity, Chief Alhaji Aminu realizes that, despite the late hour, the time has finally come to disclose the *full* story behind the horse dispute . . .

"You see, Mista Bello, when Danjuma died there was a rivalry. Who was to take the place of the old chief? Most people wanted it to be me. But Brah thought that he, as son, should take over. There was an election, conducted according to our custom." That meant assembling all of the male heads of household in the village. Then they lined up behind their preferred candidate. "In the end, I received 133 votes (even though the official paper—I'll show you—says 103). Brah got only 37. All the problems with him—including the dispute over your horse—stem from that."

The chief ducks into his hut and brings out sheaves of official Nigérien government papers, with blue-inked rubber stamps. As is typical for this former French colony, even though the only language the villagers (including the chief) understand is Hausa, the document is written less for local usage than to pass Napoleonic muster. I translate, roughly:

IN CONSIDERATION OF the Constitution of May 12, 1997;
IN CONSIDERATION OF Law number 64-023 of July 17, 1964
relating to the creation of administrative districts . . .
IN CONSIDERATION OF Regulation number 93-023/PM/MI of
March 30, 1993 relating to the status of the traditional chieftaincy
of Niger;
IN CONSIDERATION OF Decree number 93-095/PM/MI of
April 15, 1993 modifying the Regulation . . . of March 30, 1993 . . .

and in consideration of Executive Order this, and in consideration of Affidavit that, and noting that the late chief's son and the late chief's (misspelled) brother (born "around" 1950 and 1948, respectively) are both

REPUBLIQUE DU NIGER
DEPARTEMENT DE ZINDER
ARRONDISSEMENT DE MAGARIA

PROCES-VERBAL D'ELECTION DU CHEF DE VILLAGE
DE YEKOUA YARORO (CANTON DE MAGARIA)

L'an mil neuf cent quatre vingt dix neuf et le 5 Janvier, se sont déroulées les opérations de consultation de chefs de famille du village de Yékoua Yaroro (canton de Magaria) sous la présidence MAHAMAN NASSIROU BAKO SOUS-PREFET ADJOINT de l'Arrondissement de Magaria, en vue de l'élection du nouveau chef dudit village en présence de :

- MAMAN BACHIR HAROU, Wambèye Magaria
- CHADAI IBRAH HAROU
- MAMAN YERINA AMADOU, notable
- Plusieurs chefs de village et notables invités pour la circonstance

Après les salutations d'usage, le Président a pris la parole pour rappeler et expliquer à l'assistance l'importance et le rôle des chefs coutumiers dans notre pays ainsi que le mode de leur élection conformément au statut de leur association.

Afin de vérifier le nombre de présences, le Sous-Préfet Adjoint a demandé au secrétaire de séance de procéder à l'appel de chefs de famille inscrits dans registre de recensement du village.

Il ressort de ce contrôle

- Inscrits   193
- Présents   140
- Décés   17
- Absents   36

Le quorum étant largement atteint, le Sous-Préfet Adjoint a demandé à tous les ayants droit à la chefferie du village et qui sont candidats à la succession, de se présenter officiellement. C'est ainsi que deux(2) candidats se sont présentés :

1. Ibrah Adamou Mahaman fils ainé du disparu né ver 1950 à Yékoua inscrit sous le n°6 de la cate de famille

2. Elhadji Amirou Mahaman, frère du disparu né vers 1940 à Yékoua, inscrit sous le n°34 de la carte de famille n° 1

Après vérification de candidatures, le Sous-Préfet Adjoint a demandé aux candidats de se retirer pour trouver un consensus pour garder l'esprit de cohésion dans la famille. Les deux(2) candidats ont tous maintenu leurs désires de se présenter.

Après les opérations de vote le résultat inscrit suivant a été obtenu:

1°) Elhadji Aminou Mahaman   103 voix
2°) Brah Adamou Mahaman   37 voix

.../...

Comme le confirme le vote, le Sous-Préfet Adjoint a déclaré Mr. Elhadji Aminou Mahamah nouveau chef de village de Yékoua Yaroro, en remplacement de son frère Mr. Adamou Mahaman décédé.

Enfin le Sous-Préfet Adjoint et le Représentant du chef de canton ont pris la parole tour à tour pour prodiguer des sages conseils au nouveau élu et à ses administrés.

En foi de quoi, le présent Procès-Verbal a été dressé pour servir et valoir ce que de droit.

Fait à Magaria, les jours, mois et an que dessus.

LE SOUS - PREFET

New chief election record.

eligible for the chieftaincy and that neither candidate has agreed to withdraw "so as to achieve a consensus that would preserve the spirit of cohesion in the family," in two and a half pages of French bureaucratese, and with the obligatory stamps of the Assistant County Executive and signatures of the County Executive of Magaria,

"IT IS DECIDED THAT Monsieur Alhaji Aminu is named village chief . . ." How I pine for a copy of this archival treasure!

So this is the root cause of my African horse problem: a classic story of royal intrigue, here played out on the local level. Just as the death of King Hussein of Jordan pitted his brother, the Crown Prince Hassan, against the king's son, Abdullah II, so had Chief Danjuma's demise set uncle—Alhaji Aminu—against nephew—Mallam Brah. In the Hashemite Kingdom of Jordan, nephew ultimately prevailed over uncle; here, in the Nigérien village of Yekuwa, the uncle proves the victor. In Yekuwa, at least, there was an election to determine the outcome.

"Mallam Brah was angry about losing," continues the chief. "Even if he couldn't claim to become the new chief, he could at least claim the old chief's belongings. Including your horse. That's how all this trouble started. *Ka gani*? Now do you see?"

How naïve I have been—I, the supposed expert on the local scene, the political scientist! Pique and jealousy over a lost chieftaincy election in a remote Hausa village—is this why I have yanked my son out of school in wintry New England and brought him into tropical West Africa? But how else would we have discovered the village secret, if we hadn't come?

It is gratifying to have gotten to the heart of our Hausaland dilemma. But I still must confront this latest unpleasant twist: Brah's hand-delivered threat and its implied doublecross. No matter how phlegmatic are the chief and my host, I cannot afford to wait and let matters run their course. Faralu warned me about Brah's unreliability; in his own bullying scrawl, Brah has just confirmed the fears of Faralu. I decide to up the ante.

It was 11:00 at night, so our retainer, Faralu (Far-A-LU) got the keys and brought me home from the chief's hut. A retainer is a companion and helper. I brushed my teeth and fell asleep. Dad came in a few minutes later.

It is true that I have not come to "squeeze" anyone; but now Brah has forced my hand. Tomorrow we shall return to my first Hausa hometown from decades past, and I shall seek justice from a higher authority.

14

The road to Magaria was so bumpy that I was sure I'd lose my breakfast. Along the way, in the middle of the road, there was a woman walking along carrying wares on her head. Startled by our car, she started running to the right and so our driver veered to the left. Then, like a panicked bunny, she began running to the left. So the driver veered suddenly to the right and we began to swerve out of control. Just when it looked like we were heading off the road, Dad's door flew open! We didn't crash, though. All the men in the car (except Dad) started yelling and insulting the woman. With all that swerving, it was all I could do to stop myself from vomiting.

Compared with Yekuwa, Magaria is a major metropolis. True, the bank, cinema, and groundnut factory have been closed for decades; the streets are still not paved; and the one retail food store, named for the old Lebanese trader Chamchoum (is he still alive?), is all boarded up. But as a district capital, on a major thoroughfare from the provincial capital Zinder to Kano in Nigeria, Magaria still commands prestige. Trucks and jeeps rumble in and out; a few homes have electricity and running water; and there is a high school, where I spent two years growing into true adulthood as a *professeur d'anglais*. Although I had nothing to do with him during my stint as a Peace Corps Volunteer, there is a *sarki*—a paramount chief, an emir—whom I spent hours interviewing years later as a Fulbright scholar. It is only his picture, in fact—taken with sword-toting bodyguard—that my publishers accorded full-page reproduction in *Hausaland Divided*. Indeed, a principal purpose for traveling to Magaria on this trip is to present the chief with a copy of the book. Now, in addition to the offering of tome, there will be serious talk of horse.

When we finally arrived in Magaria, the first person we met was the elderly Abdu Dan Tata. He is the father of our host Mallam Souleymane Abba.

Mallam Souleymane was very lively, meaning that he had a sense of humor, laughed a lot and, although handicapped, wasn't constantly downcast. His legs didn't work properly; he got around walking with two small wooden slabs. Using these, he didn't have to use his knuckles. Instead, he used the slabs, transporting himself with his hands. I wasn't horrified at his handicap, though; in the market in Kano, on our second day in Africa, I had seen a boy walk with one hand and one foot. One of his feet, the bad one, was twisted backwards, while his bad hand was twisted in back of him. He had a sandal on each limb that he walked with. I was pretty appalled because normally, you'd think someone in this state would be in the hospital, or at least get around in a wheelchair. So when I first saw Mallam Souleymane, I wasn't too upset or revolted.

Except for Mamane, my housekeeper of Peace Corps days, I have known Souleymane longer than any other person in Africa. It is in his extended compound (shared with his father and boarding students) that we shall stay. And it is he—now holding the prestigious post of ward alderman—who will be our conduit to the Sarki, the King of Magaria.

Souleymane has the same bright wide eyes, expressive facial features, and cheery alert look I remember from over twenty years before. He unfortunately bears the same disability, and his *keke*, beginning to break down, remains his main means of transportation. For some of the sandier streets of town, he needs a couple of boys to push.

Our first house, in Yardaje, was like clay, resembling an adobe. Our second house, in Yekuwa, was square-like, similar to a camping tent. Here in Magaria, our third house is way cool. On the ceiling it's got a spider web design made of cut papers larger than I am. There are magazines on the walls, a clothes rack, an (old) radio, an atlas, and a hammock!

While the sarki's authority is intact, his palace, never sumptuous to begin with, has deteriorated from its frumpy state of over a decade ago. Dust balls hang from the rafters; several window panes are broken; some windows have no glass at all. There is a massive crack in the wall. Except for the dusty, gray chairs along one wall, the only piece of "furniture" in the reception room is a cardboard box bearing the good marketing news, "Oui, C'est un téléviseur!" Somehow, I can't imagine this aging king watching TV; his vision is so weak he doesn't even try to look at his own published portrait in my book. Fortunately, the palace does not seem decrepit to my son. He eagerly takes in the

10 men seated on the floor, wearing magnificent robes.

How easy it is to forget foreign protocol! One should not address a Hausa king directly, but rather speak softly through an intermediary who in turn repeats one's words. Mallam Souleymane is my intermediary, seated on the ground below Sam and me. Souleymane eventually guides me from book offering to horse problem.

Now Faralu arrives! Permitted entry by the numerous gatekeepers, he prostrates himself on the mat a good fifteen feet in front of the sarki. Eyes averted from the king (as befits custom) Faralu begins relating the horse story from the beginning: the agreement with Danjuma, the sale and resale of Sa'a, Brah's treachery . . .

"*Rankye dadi!* Long live the King!" declares the arriving chief of Yekuwa, Alhaji Aminu. He too prostrates himself, and then he and the King of Magaria embark on several minutes of greetings, overlaid with the voices of palace functionaries, assorted courtesans, and bodyguards. "May Allah prolong your life! May you obtain whatever you desire!" There ensues a major discussion over Mista Bello's horse, his son's inheritance, and Brah's obstreperousness.

"Faralu and Mallam Alhaji Harouna went to the *hakimi*," the chief explains, not needing to specify that the *hakimi* in Yekuwa is the King of Magaria's own son. "They showed him Mista Bello's paper. He spoke to Mallam Brah: but Mallam Brah ignored what he was told."

The king does not hear well. This is the double-edged sword of African age: enhanced prestige along with diminished capacity. Key points are repeated to him, often by several people. Many people speak at once about various aspects of my horse and me.

"Mista Bello told Mallam Brah," the chief of Yekuwa continues, "'Before we leave, I want my son to ride his horse.'" All eyes go to Sam, who is busily scribbling away in his diary.

"We know the saying," the village chief admits, embarrassed. "'If you entrust someone with so much as a pin, that pin must be returned.' As long as this matter is not resolved, bad feeling and shame will stain our village. We would like you to help us." It is an extraordinary admission and plea from the very man who is himself charged with preserving good will in the community.

Faralu continues explaining his side of the story. "Mallam Brah said, 'If I obtain the money, I will return it. But if I can't get it, then I won't give it.'"

This is not quite right. Even if Brah's prevaricating statement about partial refunds and required divine support implied this, I cannot remain silent hearing such a distorted version of my nemesis' actual words. I break in and correct Faralu's recollection, providing a more verbatim account. To "squeeze" your adversary is one thing; to permit outright misstatement of his words is another.

"Tomorrow is market day in Kwaya," says Chief Aminu. Everyone knows that Kwaya is the premier horse market for the entire region. "If Mista Bello is going to buy another horse—which he wants to do, for his son—then he needs his money by then."

As the palaver continues, more and more people in the palace weigh in with their own interpretations and advice. The din rises, obscuring the king's own words. There are repetitions and corrections of the horse sale amount, specifications of deductions for commissions and seller's fees, various versions of who said what and when, a recounting of different options to resolve the inheritance knot. My name is bandied about, but I can no longer follow every stream of the discussion. Yet I do know that no one has brought Brah's infamous nighttime note to the attention of the king. As I remove the insult-and-threat sheet from my bag, I signal to Chief Alhaji Aminu to relay its contents.

The chief faithfully narrates the message to the king, concluding, "'Now you may call for the Angel of Death.'"

"*Aph! Asha! Wayyo!*" Sarki and all his court attendants break out in onomatopoeic incredulity.

Speaking as if distracted, the king asks of no one in particular, "Is tomorrow indeed market day in Kwaya?" Several people, in unison, assure his Highness that it is so. Sarkin Magaria lowers his voice and, speaking slowly and deliberately, directly addresses Alhaji Aminu. His tone and body language are all a signal: the king is rendering judgment.

"Chief, you need to make them see reason."

"May you speak with Allah's voice," Chief Aminu responds.

"They have displayed grave lapses in truth and in trust. They know, and everyone else knows, that the horse is not their late father's. Tell them"—he pauses royally, imparting gravity and finality—"to give up the money. The horse money."

"We will tell them," Chief Alhaji Aminu affirms.

"It is an obligation." The Yekuwa chief agrees. "Furthermore," the *sarki* says, "before giving the money, they must appear before me."

Kai! The palace entourage breaks out in barely controlled pandemonium. Words of "trust" and "friendship" and "horse" and "riding" and "money" punctuate the animated discussion; so do "If Allah wills it." Again, I can no longer follow all the details, except to note that part of the hubbub revolves around the financial implications of transporting Brah to Magaria: How much will it cost, who will bear the expense? Then there is the procedural question: does Brah actually need to appear if he willingly tenders the full amount of money? The more these royal proceedings swirl around Sam and me, the less my son and I participate. We have become bit players in a high Hausa drama.

Eventually the king remembers me and, in the midst of all his Hausa speech, utters three words in French: *abus de confiance*.

"We will summon him here for *abus de confiance*—breach of trust." Then, turning to his court advisers, his Highness adds, "We shall let him know that if he doesn't obey us, he'll go to the gendarmerie, and to prison." But the king utters this last sentence with a laugh, as if he has just uttered an inside joke. Will local gendarmes really arrest a villager for *abus de confiance*? Will Nigérien legal authorities really bother about the claim to a horse in the bush by a White Man who lives in America? Probably not, but popular perception props up palace politics. Even if the king has no official power to hand over alleged horse swindlers to the gendarmes—long ago the colonial French in Niger severely undercut the chieftaincy's judicial power—peasants undoubtedly believe that he does.

Before taking leave of Sarkin Magaria, Chief Alhaji Aminu is given a convocation—a summons, handwritten in French—for Brah.

Tomorrow, here in Magaria, we should achieve some measure of closure: either horse money in hand or Brah's appearance before the king.

We will spend the night in Magaria—where exactly I'm not sure—in anticipation of the following day's outcome.

The summons.

15

"It is as if the years have disappeared." Mamane's face looks thinner, the wrinkle lines deeper. Yet the man who first initiated me into Hausa culture as my "boy" even as he catered to my petty needs as a White Man, still smiles. He has not had a salaried job since the Peace Corps pulled out of Magaria in the 1980s. But he now has a more precious status: that of grandfather.

"Look at the power of God," he tells me repeatedly. "Here we are together again. Just like in the old days. Only now, Allah has granted you a son. And he has seen you through this voyage to reunite us."

I have never inquired into Mamane's age. From the start, I assumed he was older than I—but how much older can he be? His wife, Ladi, still has the full, round face that I'd remembered; the rest of her body has amply filled out as well. As a Hausa man, Mamane has every reason to be proud of his spouse's enlarged appearance.

Mamane accompanies us from his home in the middle of Magaria to the school complex, at the outskirts of town. First we pass the site of the primary school, whose principal twenty years before accused me—in front of my alarmed father—of being a spy, all because we took a picture of the grass-hut schoolrooms added to accommodate the young student spillover. "You will surrender the film," he had ordered, incensed by his own imagined notion that we would show the entire world false propaganda about his mother country's educational infrastructure. I had to assure my visiting father that I was not in as serious trouble as it seemed. But I seethed inside.

We then pass the former residence of Zouménou, my *histoire-géographie* teacher friend from Benin, between whose house and mine we would spend entire Sundays accompanying each other home African-style, by foot, back and forth, taking long pauses in each other's abode for refreshments. It was Zouménou who, for his lesson on the ancient Near East, invited me to address his class as a modern-day descendant of the nomadic Hebrews described in the French-language textbook. It made me feel like a Lubavitcher version of Mel Brooks's Million Year Old Man. Upon completion of my Peace Corps service I'd spent a long week at Zouménou's parents' home in Port-Novo in Benin, waiting for him to return from the University of Abidjan. But Zouménou never arrived and, twenty-one years later, I still wonder what detained him.

Mamane speaks about Bobo, my highly intelligent but racist dog who had provided me constant companionship and continuous streams of puppies. Bobo, a Peace Corps hand-me-down, barked at all unfamiliar Africans and licked all visiting Americans. (Muslim townsfolk generally despise dogs—children often throw rocks at them—and Bobo knew that light-skinned humans would invariably treat her well.) My very last image of Magaria—blurry from tears—is that of Bobo running frantically after the Peace Corps Land Rover that was bringing me away for good . . .

Right now I'm at the school inspector's house. All the teachers live in one block right next to the school. The really important people like the director of health and the crop manager have the biggest houses, and the teachers have the second best (still huge, by village standards).

The schoolyard is still sandy; water troughs to slake students' thirst still stand outdoors. Not much has changed in this French West African school where, during two years two decades ago, I taught English and, despite the situational celibacy, matured into true manhood. The current high school principal digs into the archives to retrieve my original in-service sign-in entry: Even my signature as a twenty-one-year-old now appears immature.

We're going to eat over the school inspector's house. I think the inspector's daughter is trying to impress me, so I'd better do something quickly. See ya!

There is one major change in Magaria, however: a handful of the town's elite, including the school inspector, have satellite dishes and television sets. They cannot pick up Niger's own television station in Niamey, the nation's capital; they do have access, however, to Arabstat, BBC, and CNN. In the plush living room of Magaria's school inspector—who, like most members of Niger's modern élite, is not himself Hausa—I watch the results of a Republican Party primary pitting George Bush against John McCain. Commercials and schlock American shows, the likes of which I do not permit in my own home, beam into this rural West African living room. Sam is happy: in Magaria, he gets to watch the television forbidden to him in Massachusetts! I ask the inspector, who has spent most of his life in French West Africa, for his impressions of the Western world.

"We think that you are living in a dangerous country, where there is violence and there are thugs. Especially in America." Still, "Americans are very friendly. Very adaptable."

There remains an unmistakable French-like formality within the small circle of African educators in this undistinguished Nigérien town. One of the inspector's colleagues—the high school principal—drops in to exchange evening greetings.

"Bonsoir, Monsieur le Directeur."

"Bonsoir, Monsieur le Conseiller."

These are men who see each other on a daily basis.

After eating corn grinded up so it looks like solid bits of rice (with sauce) and a french fry-shaped potato called igname (IN-YAM) (with sauce), the inspector's wife put some butter made from the milk of oxen on a wound in my shoulder (I had scraped myself during a soccer game back home and the scab was beginning to peel off and hurt). It smelled real bad, but it did make my wound feel much better.

Before dinner, Sam and I use the faucet and sink in the bathroom to wash up and marvel at the convenience of a flush toilet. The delicious meal, the Western-style eating arrangements (table, chairs, plates, cutlery), and the sophisticated conversation in French (the inspector had spent some years in France) make me see Magaria with new eyes. When one comes straight from America—or even from Niamey, the capital— Magaria appears as a remote outpost, a backwater; compared with Yardaje and Yekuwa, however, it is the lap of luxury. As much as I am happy to give Sam a break from our rugged village life, I also feel vaguely guilty about reveling with a Magaria mucky-muck. I do decline, however, the inspector's suggestion that we leave Mallam Souleymane's rather primitive compound for more comfortable accommodations in his own home.

Before we take leave, the inspector hands my son a strange-looking object. He explains what it is; my son looks at me and flinches: it is a piece of elephant skin.

I asked the inspector in French: "Was this animal hunted? In the wild?" "No, it was in a game reserve and died of old age. Only after that was its skin taken." I was very relieved.

The inspector is embarrassed: he had left word with his driver (yes, the school complex now has a vehicle and chauffeur at its disposition!) that he is to drive Sam and me home, back to Soulyemane's compound on the other edge of town. But the driver does not show up. It is very dark, very late, and very far (especially for Sam). The inspector, always courteous, accompanies us half-way home and makes sure that other colleagues see us the rest of the way. On the way we speak of the importance of collegiality, institutional loyalty, and cross-cultural friendship.

We walked home zombie-like (I didn't even brush my teeth) and fell asleep. When I awoke at 4:00 AM I lost all sense of direction because, while I slept, Dad had put a mosquito net which made me think I was under the hammock. It was too dark to see, so I gave up and fell back asleep thinking that I'd find out where I was in my own house in the morning.

Our room in Souleymane's compound, furnished with paper cutouts, magazine covers, and campaign posters and ballots, is normally occupied by a couple of students from the Magaria high school. Every so often one of their friends drops in, and is startled to find, instead of his classmate, a White Man and boy. Just outside our room, in the antechambers, six young Muslim disciples, who during the mornings and evenings join scores of other children belting out Koranic verses in cacophonous unison, spend the night, fully clothed, sleeping next to each other on worn, straw mats. If home is where you sleep, this piece of ground is their home. Next to my bed, I glimpse the title of one of the occupant's books: *Les Grands Textes de la Philosophie.* Next to the disciples' "room" are tethered a bull and a sheep. The emerging worldviews of these Koranic and high school students, otherwise living cheek-by-jowl, could not be more contradictory.

After eating French bread and raw cereal and tea, we went to the market to exchange American dollars into African francs. Dad got 22,500 CFA from $50.00 to give to Mamane. Then we went to a tailor to repair a zipper on Dad's jacket. When the tailor heard us speak English he asked if we were Japanese. We said, "No. Why?" His answer wasn't very clear to me but went like this: "You said you spoke English, so I concluded you were Japanese." Hmmm.

It was awfully hot, so we went to a soda seller. I bought 7UP with a 100 CFA coin. Then the Land Rover from Yekuwa arrived.

Out pops Faralu. The Land Rover whisks away. I am impatient to know the outcome of the royal summoning of Brah. Faralu is just as impatient to tell me. But it would be undignified to begin any other way than . . .

"How did you spend the night?"

"In health."

"Have you come in health?"

"Only in health."

"How did you leave them?"

"Thanks be to Allah. How is Isma'il?"

"In health," my son also answers in Hausa, now with nary an accent.

The Magaria market is gearing up. It is so noisy that in order to converse we need to walk away from the center.

"So, Faralu, what is the news?"

Religious music blares in the background. A goat bleats; then a sheep.

Faralu, not usually partial to flowery discourse, responds allegorically. "Talk is finished," he declares with a theatrical flourish. "The fire is out!" I look at him quizzically.

"The horse money—" he says, smiling. "They've given it. It's all here." He pats his deep, bulging pocket under his long, flowing tunic.

"There is more," he says excitedly. "There is a new horse back home— Usman Gada Ya'u, younger brother of Galadima, bought it on Monday in a village along the road to Zinder. He returned to Yekuwa with it just last night. I've seen it, and so have Alhaji Mallam Harouna and the chief. Everyone says that it's truly a good one. They say you should come home and see the horse yourselves, you and Samuel. We'll put a saddle on it and Sam will ride. That's it—relief has arrived."

It sounds too good to be true: Money in hand, a scenario delivering us from traumatic trading in the horse market. But there is, of course, a problem . . .

Early on our host diplomatically had broached the financial wrinkle to our horse dilemma: inflation. Although we are technically in Niger, whose official currency is the stable West African franc backed by the treasury of France, here in the border region the economy is totally dominated by that of Nigeria and its infamously erratic naira. "Since they sold your horse," Alhaji Mallam Harouna informed me, well before Brah had shown his ugly side, "the naira has fallen. A lot. The money needed to buy a horse then will only purchase half a horse now." Alhaji Mallam Harouna's observation is borne out when I learn the price of the newly available horse: thirteen thousand naira, double what I had originally paid for Sa'a.

Could it be otherwise? Could victory truly have been so complete, that we simply replace our lost horse with the naira reimbursed by Brah and his brothers? Hardly: my Hausa entanglements are rarely so simply resolved, especially when it comes to money. Having saved face and redeemed reputation, do I now cleanly cut our losses or get even more deeply involved financially? Should I take the money and run, give it away, or reach back into my savings and spend just as much all over again, so as to restore a precarious equestrian status quo? I turn back to Faralu.

"What kind of horse is it?" I ask. "What color?"

Faralu cannot contain himself and yells out his answer. "A beautiful one!"

"You really agree with this horse?" I pursue.

"I certainly agree with this one. The chief saw it first and told me to go have a look. I went and stroked it. Stroked it all over. It's really beautiful."

I translate Faralu's words for Samuel, repeating the accolades that all and sundry are already pouring on Sam's prospective new steed. I stop in mid-translation to ask Faralu a very prosaic question.

"Faralu, did you actually mount it?"

"No, we were in a hurry."

"He didn't actually ride it," I have to tell Sam, "but Faralu's seen it and says it's a very nice horse. He, Alhaji Harouna, and the chief have seen it. They're all in agreement with that horse and think that you're going to like it."

"Then I will," declares my son, with the confidence of a young prince. Faralu is ecstatic. He says that the horse is tethered for us at the homestead of Galadima, the royal notary.

To celebrate the news that the horse problem was solved, Dad brought me to the studio of a professional photographer. Dad wanted a black-and-white picture because that's how the one of my grandfather (who died before I was born and who I'm named after) was taken when he visited Dad here twenty years ago.

Twenty-one years after he visited me, and seventeen years after he passed away, my father is still remembered in Magaria. Time after time, people ask after my mother ("How is the health of the Old Woman?"), remembering that my Dad is no more. They do not ask perfunctorily; it is essential. To know how I am they need to know how my parents are. Even now. Forever more.

For some few, there is a special reason to recall and honor my mother. But it did evoke considerable awe when, as a Peace Corps twenty-something, I received greatly cherished letters from both my parents. "What?" came the bewildered reaction. "Even your *mother* knows how to read and write?!?"

Until that moment, I hadn't given Mom's being literate a second thought.

Literacy, male and female: take it not for granted.

I dedicated *Hausaland Divided* to "two Samuel Mileses":

To the father who came to Hausaland
and to the son whom I yearn to bring.

Only now, six years after publication, is that book complete.

As we wait for the photographer to arrive, we are surrounded by the usual throng of curious kids. The crowd attracts the attention of a roving gendarme on a motorbike. For some reason (is it because we are congregated at a photo studio?) he thinks we are there to shoot a film. Authorities would have required foreknowledge of this. Having heard nothing of any authorized filmmaking in Magaria, the gendarme is suspicious.

Fearing that he will ask for our passports—still conspicuously lacking valid stamps for entry into Niger—I try to preempt visa inspection by handing over my decades-old Peace Corps discharge papers. "I used to be a Volunteer here," I explain in French, "and now I am in the Reserves." This seems to satisfy him, and I am emboldened to request a picture: my son with him on the gendarme motorcycle. The gendarme admonishes in a severe tone of voice: "Only if you send me a copy."

Time to pack and leave Magaria. Dad tried to squeeze in a tiny nap, but with the kids peeking in the house and me staring at them—which makes them run and shriek—it was near impossible.

We then went to the chief's palace to say goodbye, and then to the school. For some reason—I suppose, good faith—the principal gave me French books of vocabulary, orthography, history and geography and a Magic Eye® notebook. Mom is going to go absolutely nuts when she sees them.

We hit the road in the Land Rover until Dad gave me an option. Everyone else in the truck was going to the market in another town, called Kwaya. We could go with them or get out in The Bush and wait for them to come back.

Without a quiet spell in the empty countryside, Sam will not experience that mystical quality that so affects me in rural Hausaland. We need some outdoors time together, alone, outside the range of well-wishers, staring kids, and assorted gawkers. I ask Sam to choose between market and bush.

I chose The Bush. It was a good thing, too.

I tell the driver and Alhaji Aminu to just let us out anywhere along the dirt road. But the chief will not allow us to be left alone in the empty countryside.

"Faralu, you get out too and keep company with Mista Bello and Isma'il." Faralu is obviously disappointed to miss out on the market and I protest to Aminu, "No, the two of us will be fine." But the chief is adamant and Faralu, too, refuses to leave us alone.

It was a good thing that I chose The Bush because in the few minutes after the truck left, I really had to go to the bathroom. I found some bushes and was about to go but at that moment a girl suddenly appeared out of nowhere, walking along what turned out to be a path. (Dad tells me she was a Fulani, and that the Fulani live precisely where you think there isn't a soul around.) I moved away from the path and did it near a mango tree. There are mango trees everywhere around here.

After taking a walk we listened to nature. In so many villages, people pounded millet at a rythmatical [sic] pace, so it sounded musical. The birds and cows added music, too.

We were arriving back at our resting spot near the mango trees from our little walk when Faralu reminded us that we forgot to greet him as we approached. In Niger, it's a strong tradition to greet people on arriving by saying: Salaam Alequ. The greeted person replies Amin alequu salaam. (Amin means amen.) So we took about 10 steps back, walked back to our stop, and greeted him correctly.

Tradition is very strong in Hausaland. For example: the inheritance of a son is so strong that not even a needle can go un-inherited (much less a horse). And when Dad asked the sword-maker if he could make another knife like the one he refused to sell me, the sword-maker said that not for any amount of money would he do so; a sword like that is uniquely made for a powerful chief of the region.

Sharing is also a majorly important thing. A load of times, people gave me a ton of money just 'cause I visited them. That's what I call strong traditions and customs.

Dusk begins to fall before our Land Rover whizzes past, kicking up dust. Faralu flags it down, and the vehicle screeches to a halt. I tease Jamilu, erstwhile King Teamaker, currently King of the Motor Vehicles: "What's this now? Have *you* now become the Sarkin Mantuwa? Did you completely forget that you left a White Man and his son out in the bush? Or did you really want us to be lost and sleep out in the wilderness?" Jamilu laughs, especially at the prospect of assuming my old nickname: Sarkin Mantuwa, King of the Absent-Minded Ones.

Jamilu has often wondered: How is it that, of all the thousands of Hausa villages in Niger, Mista Bello wound up with plain old Yekuwa as

his home? What allowed us, as opposed to some other ordinary settlement, to have and befriend him? To myself, the answer sometimes comes
in Hausa, sometimes in Yiddish. Perhaps it's all just *sa'a*, luck; or, just
maybe, it's actual *beshert*, fate.

There were a lot more people in the Land Rover and there were no more
seats—Alhaji Mallam Harouna was already standing crouched in the back—
when we picked up an extra passenger with a big package. So he sat on the
hood of the truck. Not exactly safe driving. It was too late when we got home
and so we decided that I would view the horse in the morning. That way, I could
see it in full splendor.

16

"When we returned from Magaria," Chief Alhaji Aminu explains to me back in Yekuwa, recapitulating his tense encounter with Brah, "I told him, 'Mista Bello has appeared before Sarki, together with his son. The king said that you must return the horse.

"'Mista Bello displayed patience, taking our advice that he accept horse money instead. That's the reason we have come, with this paper from the sarki. But you have said that you will restore only half of the money . . .'" Brah was not easily swayed.

"'Look,' the chief reasoned further, 'it brought us honor, this White Man coming to our community. He didn't come to take anything from us. He left here thinking that, from anywhere, he could always remember the trust between us and him. Even his returning now is on account of the trust he held. He travels extensively, this White Man. But it's only here, in Yekuwa, that he bought and left a horse. It has even become a famous story. If one day he decides to buy a sheep, or a camel, he'll also do it in Yekuwa, and only Yekuwa.'"

Does the chief understand that I have traveled with my son in search not only of a horse but of a tale as well? And was the invocation of possible future livestock investments really for Brah's benefit alone?

"'. . . He has elevated us. So do not permit his heart to be broken.

"'And then there is the boy—you must not destroy his faith. He has placed his trust in his father, and Mista Bello must not leave disappointed. Especially if anything should befall him in the future . . . '

"So Mallam Brah pondered the situation. He thought about his own father. And in the end, he concluded that the right thing was to return all the money. But he did so in tears, saying 'Even if I return the money, your Man will have me thrashed.'

"I reassured him that that was not the case. I told him that you came here seeking justice, not vengeance.

"So now you have heard what transpired with Brah," Chief Alhaji Aminu says. "Let me just add this, Mista Bello." He pauses. "Between me and Allah—between me and this breach of trust—don't go back to

America with a darkened soul. I want you to return with your trust in the Hausa people restored."

"This is precisely the reason I have come," I reply.

"*Yawwa!*" he exclaims, in untranslatable affirmation. "This is what I told Mallam Brah. 'When Mista Bello heard the news of your father's death, he too was bereaved. And he understood the pain that you felt. So why are you going to hurt Mista Bello? It is the way that you hurt him that has brought this [——] upon you.'"

"This what?" I ask, unfamiliar with the word.

"*Dé-ci-si-on*," Chief Aminu repeats, using a rare French word. Even coming from a non-francophone Hausa king, a written declaration in Niger demands a Gallic pronunciation.

I tread delicately, not wishing to insult the chief, but needing to know: "Tomorrow, after my heir rides his inheritance, and assuming he is happy with it, will we put everything on paper?"

"*Hakika!*" exclaims Chief Aminu. "Assuredly! This time, Alhaji Mallam Harouna will be there, and Faralu, too. And we will also gather a number of other witnesses, because—well, you know what the world is like . . . If the document is lost, at least there will have been witnesses. One of those witnesses will be a schoolboy. Because—well, you know, Allah brings death to everyone. May God preserve us, but we must take precautions. There is also aging. If the horse gets old, then we do need to make a change, and acquire a younger one. That one, too, will be Ismail's. Do you see? You need to understand that that's the way things are done."

"I understand," I reassure him. "It was just hard at first for my son to understand. In his mind, there was only the first horse, the one that I'd described. But now he'll understand about the necessity of changing horses. As long as he and everyone knows that the replacement horse is his, be it brown, or white . . ."

". . . or chestnut," the chief adds for me, reminding me of the newly found horse's color. "With this arrangement, and with the trust you are placing in us again, may Allah erase our shame. This paper that we are going to draw up—just show it to your close friends and loved ones. When anyone of them comes here with it, Faralu will prepare the horse so that they can ride.

"Such papers can ensure longevity. It's like our old kings whom we still know about, even after five or six hundred years . . ."

Faralu, all toothless smile, guides us through the sandy streets of Yekuwa, bringing us to a compound set off by a straw fence. There, one hoof tethered to a wooden stake in the ground, alternately chomping hay and flicking away flies, is a chestnut-colored equine with five small white patches: one on the snout, one on each hoof. In no time at all, a small crowd has also gathered to make its own inspection.

Bigger than a pony, but still small for a horse, the animal signals calm alertness as we approach it.

A sweet smile forms on my son's lips. It is a smile worth traveling halfway around the world to see.

Sam puts his own face next to that of Sa'a's replacement, and gently pats the white patch on the horse's snout.

"Not too close, Sam." I'd always been warned that an innocent upward movement of a horse head could smash a human jaw up through the oral cavity. But Sa'a's replacement is no nervous nelly and rather encourages my son's petting.

"*Babu cizo,*" an onlooker calls out in approbation. "He doesn't bite. It's a healthy animal—no trouble from this one."

"What do you think, Sam?"

"This horse is perfect for me! My size, too. Size four, I think. Great!"

"Are you ready to try riding him, son?"

"By myself?"

"Don't worry, I'll be walking right alongside you."

"*A sau sirdi!*" I instruct Faralu. "Saddle it up!"

Horse blanket on rump, saddle upon blanket. Strap under belly, tie to ring on saddle. Adjust stirrup length by adjusted twisting leather strips. Bit into mouth. Toss rein over neck.

Somewhere in the recesses of my cerebellum, the precise Hausa words for all these objects have been resting, undisturbed, for years. Suddenly, the bytes associated with *linjami* awaken and spring into consciousness. "Horse bit!" I declare proudly. *Mulhin sirdi*: "Saddle blanket!" It must sound strange to my village acquaintances to hear me preen in this way: "What's the big deal? Mista Bello has always known all about *kayan doki* (horse equipment)." Yet for me it feels as if a veil of amnesia is lifting and I am emerging, if ever so slowly, from a cultural coma.

As with true memory loss and recovery, however, the recall is imperfect and frustrating. Is "reins" *kamazuru* or *kazamuru*? Vocabulary percolates up through the subconscious, but imparts limited confidence to the re-acculturizing ego.

As Sam is hoisted up on the horse for the very first time, I suggest that he say the *shehechiyanu*, the Jewish prayer associated with hallowed first doings: "Blessed are You, Lord our God," Sam recites in Hebrew, from the saddle of his inheritance in this obscure village in the hinterland of West Africa, "who grants us life and sustenance, and has permitted us to reach this moment—*lazman hazeh*."

"It is our Bismillahi," I explain in Hausa to the gathering onlookers, referring to the opening line in the Muslim profession of faith. It too is commonly recited at non-liturgical moments, such as at the beginning of a journey or when sitting down to join conversation.

"Dad, this is really good. He obeys really well!"

"Pat him, so he really knows who you are."

Someone calls out in Hausa. "He should ride it all the way to Kano! Or to America!" There is good-natured laughter all about. "That's precisely what my son would like," I reply. "But if he can't, I guess we'll leave it here."

Sam: "How will we ride together, Dad?"

Me: "I'll borrow the town crier's horse."

Sam: "Oh, 'Dappled Gray.' That will be great."

A villager schooled in such matters begins to teach Sam horse clucking sounds: to go, to stop, to relax. Do not ask if this is a universal language, or a vocabulary understood only by horses in Hausaland. Only this I aver: Sam catches on quickly.

"Sam, what do you want to name him?"

"Let's give him the same name as the original horse, Dad—Sa'a. Luck!"

When we first arrived in Yekuwa, we tried to retrieve an enormous woven basket—bigger than me—that Dad had buried last time he was here. When we found and opened it, we discovered an odd assortment of things: a gas lamp, pots, pans, a spoon and two forks, cups, and a mousetrap. When we took some of these items out, I couldn't have been more surprised when three mice came scrambling out. Dad started to hop around in delighted astonishment, laughing. While more things were taken out of the basket, more mice came pouring out! The ironic thing was, there was a mousetrap in a bag that was full of mice, and not one mouse was injured by it! Al Haji Malam Haru, Dad's friend, caught one and exhibited it for us to see, holding the mouse by the tail. He then swung it around his head and threw it over our wall. Most escaped with our help, but some were smart enough to scurry under the door and into the street. That incident kept us laughing for quite some time.

"Don't think that he has returned on account of money or property," Harouna rebukes the women survivors of Danjuma, as they reluctantly return the large woven basket containing all the possessions I had entrusted to the late chief. "With the airplane money that he 'killed' to come see us again, he could have bought five horses." I can't help correcting my friend's mathematics. "Actually, ten horses."

I've had a breakfast of sweetened chestnut puree, tea, and bread. The town crier asked for the leftovers of our bread from Magaria, the empty container of puree, and the rest of my tea. Later, Dad explained that villagers did not even have bread, metal containers, or tea.

17

"They let them go." Alhaji Mallam Harouna looks un-characteristically dejected as he greets us in the morning. As is his wont during these dusty, cold season mornings, he has wrapped a checkered Arabian scarf around his throat. "They shot the innocent Muslim all those times and now they walk free." He shakes his head, bewildered.

Even as my Hausa host and I are having this discussion, back home my wife is panicking. Shortly after Sam and I set off on our journey, religious riots broke out in Kaduna, the city in northern Nigeria where I had interned during a summer for the State Department. Just as northern Nigerian governments are legislating the adoption of shariah, Islamic law, Christian missionaries are accused of proselytizing Muslims in Kaduna. Mosques and churches are burned to the ground; thousands of people are killed. In America, this is the news from Africa: Nigerians are killing one another in a holy war. My wife fears that her unsuspecting, obviously foreign husband and son may be mistaken for missionaries and targeted in the mass hysteria and blood-letting.

But Alhaji Mallam Harouna—who is as disgusted by the riots as any level-headed person—is not talking about them now. Over the Hausa service of the Voice of America he has just heard the verdict in the Amadou Diallo case: the young immigrant from Guinea who was fatally gunned down by four plainclothes New York City policemen. My Hausa preacher friend does not understand how men who kill an obviously innocent other—a religious Muslim, no less—can be found, prosecuted, and then released without punishment.

It is no secret in the village that I hail from New York. Yet Alhaji Mallam Harouna does not ask me to explain the Diallo verdict. I am his guest; he will not put me on the spot. From our peaceable African village home, together we quietly rue the insanity and danger of life in that faroff, mysterious land called America. For the moment, the fatal shots ringing out late at night in that dark stairwell in Manhattan are much closer, and more upsetting, to the two of us than is the rioting in nearby Nigeria, another kind of lunacy that back home, night after night, is robbing my overwrought wife, mother of Sama'ila, of sleep.

He's a little disobedient but I like my new, reddish brown horse for a multiple of reasons. He's my size, which is a little bigger than a pony. Another reason is his speed. He has a tuft of hair on each side of his leg muscle. The Hausas claim that in their land, those tufts of hair are like wings. Horses who have them fly with swiftness. I'm not sure of other horses, but for this one, it's true!

We are not what we eat: we are what we read. To explain my lust for travel and adventure to friends, I always invoke the same boyhood favorites: *Treasure Island*, *Tom Sawyer*, *Huckleberry Finn*, *Robinson Crusoe*, *The Swiss Family Robinson*. But now, recalling the image of American son meeting African horse, I realize that another classic has also subliminally stunted my full passage into staid adulthood: *Black Beauty*.

I have named my horse Sa'a (SA-AH) because that was the name of my Dad's horse. In Hausa it means Luck.

A day before our leaving Yekuwa, I still cannot stop thinking about Aminu's official chieftaincy certification, the Nigérien government documentation of his village electoral landslide. I long for a copy—not just a transcription, but an authentic reproduction of this unique historical record. I cannot shake the incongruity that this paper incarnates: fulsome and officious French to sanction a chiefly succession deep in the African bush.

I do not dare ask Chief Aminu to borrow his proof of title and mail it back from America. Alhaji Harouna has a much simpler suggestion: Why not have one of the villagers go to the county capital and make a copy there? The pharmacy, everyone knows, has a photocopier.

Xerox in Magaria? Has so much progress been made in southcentral Niger? It sounds like a wonderful suggestion, all the more since Ma'aru Tangu is planning to travel to Magaria anyway. Having spent a few years in school, Tangu knows some French and is therefore a sophisticate in the ways of the modern world. I give him some scarce French West African francs (unlike Yekuwa, Magaria really is part of the Nigérien economy) to make a copy of the chieftaincy title. He should get back later that afternoon.

Tangu does not return.

Here are the major things that are going to happen today: siesta now, horseback riding in the afternoon. Bye! (My stomach hurts so I don't want to write anymore.)

How many times will Sam actually ride Sa'a? Tomorrow we need already begin our journey back to America. I can borrow the horse of the *hakimi*, or that of Jagga the town crier, and together we may ride. Our father-son Sahelian horse rides will be memorable though few.

We rode to the outskirts of the village followed by a billion kids. Dad then borrowed my horse to go riding in the desert.

When we rode back into the village, we came upon a wedding party. There was a huge *crowd and the drummers kept up a steady beat. Then the crowd parted to make room for our two horses to pass in between. Everyone started chanting and clapping and the drummers joined in: "Mis-tah Bello!* (boum boum boum) *Mis-tah Bello!* (boum boum boum)" *Then we rode back through the passage in the crowd and a* zillion *people touched my leg and tried not to let me know it. Even some adults did! But the adults tried to look less guilty, even though I saw them.*

There is a fine line between crowd ecstasy and rioting. We are straddling this line right now. All this cheering, chanting, and drumming is intoxicating: "Mista Bello! (boum-boum-boum). Mista Bello! (boum-boum-boum)." But please, God, don't let Sa'a cut loose with Sam and trample anyone!

When we were about to leave the wedding party, some (bleeeep) kids hit my horse's rear and urged him on to gallop. He did. But I managed to hold Sa'a, and turned him around. Then I got the last laugh. The kids thought I was mad (and I was) and that I was going to run them over. But of course I wouldn't . . .

When we returned home and got off our horses, my legs were really wobbly. After our bath I tripped over the bench I wanted to put my clothes on and turned over the gas lamp. Dad fixed it but at first he was mad at me because he thought I'd broken it. With my big sandals, I am so clumsy.

Even on this momentous day, joining son with horse and successfully riding duo out in the West African bush, I am a flawed father: I yell at Sam for not watching where he puts his feet. Later I shall apologize, and he shall forgive me, breaking my heart as he blames himself for his clumsiness. Why cannot I not be more like my own father, who never raised his voice at me?

After a dinner of couscous, beans and tuna I went to bed and forgot to brush my teeth. Whoopsies!

With Sam in bed, it is time to attend to the financial necessities of our new horse. No one has told me what I need to do or by when or how: it is assumed that I know. Even after all these years, I "pass" too well. My Hausa friends assume that I remember the customs better than I actually do. Yet the passage of time liberates me, too: I shall create my own customs.

"Please call for the Chief of the Blindmen's Village Council," I ask my host. Several hours later Alhaji Mallam Harouna informs me, "Their official leader is traveling just now. Let me try to find their replacement."

In Yardaje, even the blind men—after all, they *are* Nigerian—are more assertive than their shy counterparts in Yekuwa, Niger. In Yardaje the King of the Blindmen came on his own to my compound to request that I intercede for his group with the United Nations itself; here in Yekuwa, I practically have to stuff naira into the pockets of the acting representative of the village blind. "This is my *lada*, the commission I need to give as purchaser," I explain to my bemused imamic friend. "You have witnessed it. When I give the owner of Sam's horse his money, you can say that I have already accounted for the *lada*.

"And this," I bemuse Alhaji Mallam Harouna even more, handing him a handful of naira after the bewildered blind man is led away, "is for Mallam Brah. It is *ku'din wanke kumya*." Although the phraseology is quintessentially Hausa, for all I know I am inventing both idiom and ritual. *Ku'din wanke kumya*: "money to wash away the shame." My shame. The mutual shame between Brah and Bello. A token offering to show that I bear my erstwhile nemesis no ill will. By accepting even these few naira Brah will be acknowledging that, for his part, he too forgives Mista Bello. The slate will be wiped clean.

"Let us go now to the compound of Chief Alhaji Aminu," I tell my host, "and ask to meet with the seller of the new horse."

"I have brought trouble to the community," I apologize, "and for that I am truly sorry."

"There is nothing to feel bad about," the chief replies.

"But yes—on account of me, there has been disputation in the village. There has been fighting. There have been hard feelings."

"It is not your fault."

"Still, I hope that you forgive me. And forgive me, too, for the fact that

I cannot converse in the manner that I used to. Hausa now comes to me with difficulty. I let too many years pass before returning to see you. I make too many mistakes in my speech. For that also I apologize."

"It is all right."

There is very little moonlight but not a single Chinese "hurricane" lamp, the ubiquitous lantern lighted in more affluent African settlements: nighttime illumination remains a frivolous luxury in Yekuwa. Why "burn" money on kerosene? Why use up scarce naira on batteries? All of us, seated in a circle on mats laid on the sandy ground, know each other intimately, even in the dark: Chief Alhaji Aminu; my host Mallam Harouna; Faralu, the groom; King Teamaker–turned–King of the Motorcars, Jamilu; Galadima the royal notary; Kaiga the single-toothed prince.

These are the moments I most cherish in Hausaland: sitting outside in the quiet night air, no distractions, just a few friends discussing the village day, pondering world events (as recounted in Hausa by the BBC and Voice of America) and reinforcing our human solidarity by sheer congregation. Except for nearby Yardaje there is no other community in the world where I can casually and routinely sit down with half a dozen men who care as intensely about the health and welfare of my family and myself as here in Yekuwa. It is not that I am anti-social at home: I work in a generally friendly university department, live in an amiable enough suburban neighborhood, and belong to a genuinely warm religious congregation. But here in Hausaland there exists a communal bonding that I have not experienced in other places where I have sojourned: not in the Caribbean, not in the South Pacific, not in India, not in the Indian Ocean. Not even in Israel. This bonding is based not on shared class or education or religion. Its core is rather a constant and unqualified embrace of the human condition, actualized through the repeated miracle of "seeing and being seen," and undergirded by an abiding belief in the dignity of life.

I fully appreciate the irony: I am so thoroughly accepted here *precisely* because I am an anomaly, a White (and therefore rich) Man from a greatly distant but widely admired country. But skin color and Americanhood do not guarantee my place in this corner of Muslim Black Africa; for sure, neither does being Jewish. I have *earned* my friendships in Hausaland, even if the basis of such friendship—mastery of the Hausa language—has painfully deteriorated with the passage of time.

"You will remember that I have returned with my son for three reasons," I try to perorate. "To see you and be seen. To pay condolences on the old chief's passing. And to ensure that my heir has his horse. We have fulfilled our purposes for coming and, now, we need only tie up loose ends. Tomorrow, we begin our return to America."

"May you travel in safety."

"*Amin*. I leave in happiness and in sadness. In happiness, because all is settled for my son. But in sadness, too, because I do not know when I shall next return."

"Next time, you should bring your entire family," comes a voice from the darkness.

"'The fault of the visitor,'" recites another aphoristically, "'lies in his leaving.'"

"Once again," I continue, needing to bring the conversation back to business, "I wish to leave the horse in the hands of the chief—the new chief, Alhaji Aminu . . ."

"May it be Allah's will."

". . . under the same conditions as before. 'It is his to ride as he sees fit. If the horse becomes ill, or dies, he is not to be held at fault. But when I return—or when Sama'ila returns in my place—then the horse will still be here for us.'"

"Or for Arielle, your daughter. Or for Loïza, your wife." The chief then expands on the horse-based hospitality. "If *any* of your friends come to Yekuwa to visit, they too may ride the horse. You tell them that. They just come with the paper from you and when they show it to us, they too will be free to ride. All of your family, all of your brothers, all of your friends— they are all welcome here in Yekuwa."

"*Na gode*," I respond in thanks. "And now I understand that a time may come when it is necessary to sell this horse, and buy another."

"Yes, yes, if it becomes lame or too old."

"There is no blame in it," I acknowledge.

"Ah hah! Now you understand." Before extracting and handing over to the royal notary the pre-counted piles of naira to publicly consecrate the sale, I again pose the question, delicate for my near monopoly on local literacy: "Should we put this all down on paper?"

"Yes, for sure, Mista Bello," Chief Alhaji Aminu insists. "*Ya kamata*. It's a must."

"It didn't really help last time," I say, half jokingly.

"Oh, that was different," the chief says, with a dismissive wave. "The old chief really wasn't wise to the ways of formality. But with me you have nothing to fear—and everyone here is a witness, too. You needn't worry about the paper being lost or forgotten or disregarded. But we do have to write things down, Mista Bello, because—well, you know Allah. One day, without warning, He will take you. Or me. We don't know when it will be. That's why it's better that we do make up a paper."

I take out pen, paper, black sheet of carbon, and script:

Today, Friday, the 13th day in the month of Zelkida, that is to say the 25th day in the month of February 2000, I Mista Bello, also known as William F. S. Miles, have bought a chestnut brown horse with five white spots from the hand of Galadima Ya'u. The 'cowry shells' I have paid amount to one thousand and three hundred naira, plus five hundred naira in commission that I have given to the blind men of both quarters of Yekuwa.

This horse I leave in the hands of Chief Alhaji Aminu, until the day that I—or my heir Ishmael, also known as Samuel Binyamin Miles, or my heir Arielle Pooshpam Miles—demand it.

I am instructed to include my wife in the deed, and duly insert her name and title, *uwargida*—"senior wife and mother of the household."

The name of the horse is Sa'a, even if it is exchanged on account of old age, illness, or any other contingency. Any horse that replaces this one remains the property of Mista Bello and his heirs. Death of horse is regarded as an act of God. But all efforts will be made to keep this particular horse in good health.

Under one column, I, the seller, and the chief sign; on the other side of the deed, three adult witnesses scratch their signatures. It is late, and a young teenage boy is sleeping soundly on the ground. Alhaji Aminu wakes him up. "Who knows what will happen to us?" the chief says, putting all six previous signatories in the same generational category. "We need a youth, someone who will be here after we are all gone, to witness what we are doing." So a final name and signature are affixed: "Nura Aminu."

After I read out loud the document and witness names, my companions point out that there is an omission. I agree. And so I add to the final line of the horse deed: "Faralu is the caretaker of the horse, the one called Sa'a." Faralu, for his part, insists that I draft yet another document. He dictates, and I print:

I, Faralu—the caretaker of Mista Bello's horse—greet Loïza. I greet her wholeheartedly! May Allah bless and assist her while Mista Bello and Samuel are away. We thank her . . .

to which Chief Aminu has me add his own salutation, and a word to my daughter: "The entire community of the chief, one and sundry, greet her." *Shi ke nan. Alhamdu lillahi.* That is all. Praised be Allah!

18

For breakfast very early this morning I had chocolate and matzah and (like every other morning) tea. After that I fell asleep again, until Dad started to pack. We're going back to Yardaje, and all our luggage is going by Land Rover. Dad I and I will go by horseback, me on Sa'a, Dad on the horse of the hakimi. *I am almost positive I'm going to have to stop a hundred and three times. I'm going to wear long pants, socks, sandals, and a tee shirt. Today will not be too hot, because there's a ton of foggy harmattan blocking out the sun.*

Now that there is motorized transport between Yardaje and Yekuwa, only extremely poor folk still travel between the villages by foot or donkey. Only our closest village friends understand why I prefer to return to Nigeria with my son on horseback. But do even they truly understand why I wish to subject Sam and myself to this searing eight-mile trek through the empty bush?

After we packed our stuff I found a praying mantis. I played with it until our host got up and made a (long) speech . . .

"When you arrived in Niger last week," Alhaji Mallam Harouna begins, in the formal style that is not in the least belied by the at-home and remote-village setting, "I prayed that you arrive in health and peace and would return in health and peace. Now that you are starting your journey home, I pray that this has indeed been the case." I reassure our host.

"At first," Harouna continues, "we knew only you, Mista Bello. Then you returned with your wife, Loïza. And now, we have gotten to know your son, Isma'il. Please translate for him." I comply.

"This house is also now your home," my Muslim priest friend says to my son. "It is yours to return to, on your own, even without your father. Tell this to your sister, as well—she too has a home in Yekuwa. Even when your father is gone, even when I am gone: this is your home."

It is hard to overestimate Alhaji Mallam Harouna's influence on the community. A religious reformer—some would call him a fundamentalist—he is committed in the name of Islam to changing ages-old African practices among his own homefolk. In *Hausaland Divided* I devote eleven pages to his arrest and imprisonment for "unlawful" preaching, much of it condemning both the libertine tendencies of, and the unfair burdens on, married women: "Wives wander around the village and the market for no purpose. Their husbands send them into the bush to collect firewood, or to the wells to draw water for them. Allah does not like this."

Given all the social modesty that Muslim women are supposed to display, I was initially stunned to note casual toplessness in outdoor residential areas and other open work spaces, such as threshing fields. But this was only paradoxical from a Western framework of female erotica: a Hausa woman will be much more prim about covering her legs than her American counterpart. Living in Yardaje and Yekuwa I oft beheld, in feigned nonchalance, the naked chests of my female neighbors. Indeed, on more than one early morning before donning the glasses that correct my short-sightedness, I was able to recognize and greet the guileless young wife of my next-hut-neighbor only because of the distinctive and familiar shape of her ample breasts.

No longer, it seems. Not only are Yekuwa women much less likely to bare their breasts outdoors, but the heads of a few village girls are now being covered by the telltale black headscarves of the global Muslim renaissance. Alhaji Mallam Harouna is undoubtedly the prophetic shaper of village piety. One question to avoid: How does Mista Bello fit into his host's theology?

"I will come to see you off in Yardaje tomorrow," Alhaji Mallam Harouna assures me, "before your departure for America. But Jamilu will not come." And why will the erstwhile King of the Teamen—who reminded me yesterday of a long-forgotten anecdote of my father warning me, long after I had grown into manhood, "Don't burn your tongue on the hot tea!"—not come? "He fears that, seeing you depart for America, he will shed tears. He doesn't want to disturb your spirit, and he doesn't want to make you cry, either."

An old friend with red, kola nut–stained teeth (but whose teeth here aren't stained red?) has made the pilgrimage to Mecca. Before we leave he wishes to give me a present, something he has brought back all the way from Saudi Arabia. "Do you know what this is?" he asks, hopeful. "Do you know how to use it?" The alhaji is proud to possess this sleek, cool, exotic object. At the same time he is embarrassed that he doesn't know what to do with it himself.

"Yes, I am familiar with this thing," I tell him. "It also exists in America." He is all the more proud. It is he who had given us the wild bush kitten that had wound up savaging our apartment in Boston. Will we transport another of his unique offerings all the way to America?

This time I decline the gift. I think it will be for the better if we leave it here in Yekuwa, this rare, virtually unused, tube of toothpaste.

We load the vehicle and say separate goodbyes to the two chiefs of Yekuwa ("May Allah be with you. Travel in health. Greet them, greet them all!"). Alhaji Aminu apologizes as he hands me naira for my wife: "I wanted to buy her a calabash lid but couldn't. Take this money and apply it to one of the lids you bought in the market.") Jagga, the town crier, removes his Pancho Villa–like Fulani straw hat and fixes it on my son's head. "Medicine against the sun," he declares. We stop at the palace but the *hakimi* is away.

I was really concerned about riding Sa'a for such a long distance. I asked Dad to let Faralu walk along with us, just in case. But Dad said we'd be fine.

Solitary horse riding between Yardaje and Yekuwa encapsulated my village life along the Hausaland borderland. Sam, I have decided, must have this experience as well. And we must do it alone. He must see that I can protect him, even when each of us is upon a different horse and there is no one else in this vast, empty countryside to rely on.

The children tagged alongside us until we got beyond the outskirts of the village. After a bit, we passed women pounding millet with giant mortars. One of them had her baby in a sash on her back. They greeted us in their customary manner by yelling out a very high pitched sound.

"Let's sing, Sam!" At the top of our lungs, we serenade the Sahelian wilderness with English songs and Hebrew ditties. Every so often a perplexed African appears out of nowhere. A wobbling Yardaje-bound man easily overtakes us on his bicycle. I feel foolish. This is a technology gap I hadn't considered before: pedaled two-wheelers as superior to four-legged equines.

After a while, we came across another group of women who greeted us in the same manner. But these were Fulani, and on their heads they were carrying faggots of dry branches. There were also other Fulani women carrying stacks upon stacks of bowls on their heads. They were walking to the village to sell their curdled milk. After they surrounded and greeted us in the traditional manner they asked Dad for twenty naira. Dad actually did give them money, one of them women taking it with two hands. Their gratefulness hurt our ears.

Lubricate, lubricate. Give unto strangers, and they shall give to others.

Strangers will even give to you. Cut loose from this anal Western instinct to keep your money to and for yourself.

The trip was long and slow and hot and Sa'a's rocking motion made me sleepy. My chin nodded to my chest and I fell into a trance and didn't wake up until Dad warned me that Sa'a was getting too close to his horse. Then Sa'a gently prodded me back to sleep.

After about three hours we glimpse ahead the outline of the two make-shift structures constituting the Nigérien customs station. I can't be sure that the same suspicious uniformed agent who originally let us cross into his country, by Land Rover and in the company of other Nigériens, will necessarily let us out, alone and on horseback. Nor can I even assume that the same agent will be on duty. Anxiety builds with each cantering step. This is the final border-crossing risk I need to take with my child. It is mid-afternoon, the hottest part of the day, and therefore, I gamble, the agent ought to be asleep in the little straw hut next to the official customs station. We amble up to and then trot past the *Poste de Douanes.*

"Why don't we stop at the customs station, Dad?"

"Shh." A twisted proverb forms in my head: "Let sleeping *douaniers* lie." But instead I answer, as quietly and as nonchalantly as I can, "We shouldn't disturb the man's siesta."

How can I not think of the ongoing crackdown along our own desolate southern border with Mexico, and the redoubled efforts of the U.S. Border Patrol and Immigration and Customs Enforcement (ICE) to flush out "coyotes" and their smuggled illegal alien clients? Is it not serious business, this crossing of international boundaries without proper papers? In blithely strolling across the border and violating both Nigérien and Nigerian immigration law, I know I am placing us in legal jeopardy. This is, in American terms, an unwarranted risk.

But this is *not* an American context. An American mindset would not have permitted this scenario in the first place: "smuggling" my pre–bar mitzvah son across a West African boundary on top of his replacement horse inheritance. And yet nothing else I have done as a father has ever felt so right . . .

These are the ways of a world that I have been privileged to enter. I can do no less than impart these ways to my own son. From far, far away our family was wronged. Out of principle, we have crossed continents to correct that wrong. Other good people—of another faith, color, and culture—have aided us in our quest for justice. We have resolved the matter peaceably, equitability, and honorably. Our African friends wish us only well and are praying for our safe passage home. In the hinterland of Hausaland, I remind myself, thoughts of ICE-like enforcement are inappropriate . . .

A few minutes later we arrive at the fetish of my earliest research: the ten-foot-tall iron pole sticking out of the desolate sand-and-bush scenery. It is one of many incongruous boundary markers thrown up by white colonials at the turn of the century to separate the British colony of Nigeria from French-controlled Niger, and which continue in their symbolic way to divide the two independent republics, formally and legally, from each other. But this particular pole is special. It is the one past which I have ridden countless times in my travels between Yardaje and Yekuwa. This is my personal borderline. With sad nostalgia, I now realize that the era of my crossing it by horseback is forever gone. *Lokaci ya wuce*: its time has passed.

"Do brides still ride horseback from their homes to that of their grooms?" I'd recently asked, recalling a vivid custom I witnessed years before in Yekuwa but which had already been abandoned in Yardaje as primitive and un-Islamic. The brides were dressed in garish, outlandish clothing (including oversized sunglasses), shared the horse's rump with a younger sibling, and were accompanied by a boisterous parade led by fast-beating drummers. "No," came the reply to my query about one of the most intriguing village scenes I'd ever witnessed: *Lokaci ya wuce*; its time has passed.

Sam nudges Sa'a forward between a bramble and the pole so that, aloft on his horse's rump, he is still in Niger even as Sa'a's neck and head protrude into Nigeria. I snap a picture and, as I do so, my son proudly calls out "Hausaland Divided!" He thereby invokes the title of my book whose dust jacket and frontispiece carry pictures, taken half a dozen years before he was ever even conceived, of this same boundary pole. "The world is like a pregnant women," goes one Hausa proverb. "You never know what will eventually emerge."

Once we were within sight of Yardaje, we began, once again, to be followed. A few of the annoying kids hit the horse's rear, making it buck. (Sa'a wasn't trying to throw me off, though, I'm sure.) Anyway, he wasn't high enough for me not to be able to hold on to his front bump.

We make a point of stopping at the Yardaje customs station to assure the head agent that we have returned safely from our excursion in Niger. No one asks why, if we left in one vehicle, we are returning on two horses.

The customs agent is embarrassed about the misspelled word ("boarder") on the station signboard and—on the grounds that photographing border stations violates regulations—resists my entreaties to take a picture of the sign and the Nigerian flag. He relents only after I promise not to publish the photo. As when we left his country—and as when we entered Niger—we are never asked to show visas, passports, or IDs.

Here is the other side to African bureaucracy: only unknown individuals need documents and identification papers. Unlike in the West, what matters here is not what papers you are carrying but who you are. Written proof of identity is necessary for the stranger, the suspect, the unknown. If you *are* known, having to show formal paper proof is not only superfluous; it is downright demeaning. From a narrowly legalistic American perspective my travel intentions were indeed predicated on technical illegalities: unregulated money changing and illegal border crossings. But from deep within Africa—on the borderline and with the bureaucracy—our actions are entirely appropriate. Here in Hausaland, it is wetback-and-ICE thinking that is out of whack.

We arrived in Africa bearing an even more alien concept: that you could be emotionally attached to a given animal. Even to a horse. Somehow, we have managed to cross that cultural divide as well.

19

It is eerily calm as we traverse Yardaje. Today's four-hour solar pounding has not ended, and most villagers are still in siesta mode. We are stared at by the few who have stirred. Our arms are burnt red from the sun and singed by the Harmattan: we have taken nearly four hours to make the usual ninety-minute trip. Who voluntarily goes out in the mid-day sun? Mad dogs and Englishmen. Who still travels by horseback when motorcars are available? Mallam Beel and his son Sama'ila.

When the horse was calmed (and I was done giving reproving glares at the kids) we got our stuff and put it in our house.

We'd been well advised to leave nothing behind in our Yardaje hut: not even our mosquito netting is left in the window frames. There is no water in the *tukunya*. There is, however, one unexpected addition to our compound: a man. In our absence, a roving visitor from another village has been put up in our chiefly quarters. "Oh, don't worry about the *bako*, the guest," I am reassured. "He only sleeps in the antechambers. Won't disturb you a bit."

Our supplies have not yet made it from Yekuwa. We are exhausted, thirsty, and hungry—hours behind lunchtime. But children and adult well-wishers already begin to press eagerly into our compound. The poor visitor in the antechamber is crowded into a corner. Sam just wants to be left alone, and to eat something.

I try, impossibly, to balance hospitality to well-meaning greeters with privacy for my famished son. But every other minute another neighbor enters the courtyard to welcome us back to the village. I try to head the well-wishers off at the compound entrance so that Sam is left alone. "*Barka da zuwa!* Greetings upon your return! Have you arrived back in health? How are they whom you visited?"

"*Lafiya*," I reply obligatorily. "In health."

Then, from the hut, a plaintive cry in English: "Dad, I'm hungry."

I excuse myself and rush back to assure Sam that I'm taking care of things. "We've sent for the kerosene stove," I tell my son. I don't tell him that we have nothing to cook on it.

"*Barka da zuwa!*" Another call from the compound entrance. I rush back to keep the next well-wisher away from the hut itself so that my exhausted Sam is not stared at. "*Kun dawo? Lafiya lau?* You've returned? In health?"

Intellectually, I understand that it constitutes an outright lapse in etiquette for a neighbor *not* to come greet us after our return from a neighboring village. I *must* be polite. But there is also my boy in the hut . . .

"Dad, I'm *still* hungry!"

During one of the innumerable sprints between hut and compound entrance I stop to take a needed swig from a water bottle we had left behind. But the clear, sticky liquid numbs my cheeks and mouth. Kerosene! I had forgotten to label the container of our stove and lantern fuel supply. What have I done to myself?

"Dad, what's the matter?"

"Greetings!" Now the call from the compound door is in English. This is highly unusual. Reassuring my son that I have not fatally poisoned myself (even as I fret over the effect of kerosene on internal organs), I trudge over to see who is greeting us in this alien manner. I unlatch the door. To my astonishment, there sits a four-wheel drive vehicle bearing the insignia of a Katsina State development project funded by the European Economic Community. A well-dressed Nigerian introduces himself. "We have heard that you are doing a study," he goes on, smiling, in precise, school-learned English. "Perhaps we may discuss matters of interest."

How he heard about us, I do not know. What he is doing in Yardaje, I haven't the faintest. I know that I cannot afford to alienate a roving government civil servant; but neither is this the moment to simulate a Voice of America program in Special English. My son is griping, my stomach is rumbling, my mouth is stinging; and suddenly I am asked to transform the compound into an English conversation salon. As politely as I can, I break off from the EEC's field manager to rinse out the kerosene from my throat yet again and to assure my son that everything, as always, is under control.

Now Sidi arrives. Sidi is a long-standing friend who, on account of his infirmary activities—performing vaccinations—I've nicknamed *Mai-Allura*, the Needle Man. Sidi is not someone I can perfunctorily dismiss with a return greeting or two. I usher him into our compound.

"*Sannu!* You are well? I hear you have returned on horseback. Here is something for you and Sama'ila." From the folds of his long tunic Sidi removes a half dozen chicken or guinea fowl eggs. As soon as the stove arrives, we can eat. God bless Sidi . . .

Dad made really *scrambled eggs. He made it so you couldn't physically sepa-rate egg white from egg yolk. And, of all things, it was good!*

We are brought more gifts. "What is this, Dad? Is it that Papua New Guinea thing?"

"No, Sam. It's a papaya."

After eating I went outside and sat down next to Sa'a, watching and then petting him. Dad started to film me but all the kids wanted to be in the video so they got in front of the camera. So I went home to read and do some writing. I didn't realize that the kids had made their way inside until they were practi-cally in the house. I "herded" them but forgot to lock the door. I started writing again, but again they got in. I herded them out again and this time locked the door. They started to scream and one kid climbed the wall and said "Give me 5 naira!" I told him "Shut up!" and, not understanding what I had said, he an-swered "Yes, yes." Figures.

Later that afternoon who should arrive, exhausted and sheepish, but Ma'aru Tangu—he who had disappeared with the original Yekuwa chieftaincy title! Tangu has both an intriguing tale to tell and an oral invoice to present. Have there ever been such international complica-tions in the entire history of photocopying?

"The electricity was down when I arrived in Magaria," Tangu begins, relating a common happenstance in "modern" Africa. "So I decided to go to Babura, because I know that there's a government office there that also has a photocopier." Tangu doesn't bother to mention that Babura is on the other side of the border, in Nigeria "But it was the weekend, so no-body was working."

"So the next thing was to go to Daura." Tangu of Niger takes quite the initiative. Daura, as a district capital in Nigeria, is supposed to have many modern amenities. "But by the time I arrived it was already nine o'clock at night. There was no electricity in town, either. There were just kerosene lamps, all along the streets.

"Luckily, I ran into a woman who knows all about photocopying. But she needed motorcycle money to go and get it done. Since I only had the 'French' money you gave me, though, we had to first change the CFA into Nigerian currency. Only then could I give her naira to pay for the copies and for her ride on a motorcycle to the hospital. That's where she knew to photocopy. I waited behind for her, at her office.

"By the time she returned, it was impossible to get transport back home. So I had to spend the night in Daura, at a hotel." At each step in

Tangu's saga, I silently estimate the additional "unforeseen cost" for the few pages of photocopying I had originally asked him to do. "Of course, I also had to eat.

"I knew you would have left Yekuwa by then so the next day I went to the Daura motorpark and got transport leaving me off at the Yardaje junction. I walked the rest of the way." That would have been a three-mile walk under a blistering sun.

What can I do but commiserate with Ma'aru Tangu's misfortunes and compliment him on his persistence? He has no notion of financial proportionality and never envisioned aborting his mission for Mista Bello. I act as if I am quite pleased with all the initiative he has taken on my behalf—and on my tab.

In addition to the expenses he has already incurred, I must pay for Tangu's transport back to Yekuwa and, of course, give him money for his *wahalla*—his trouble, travails, and tribulations.

All sums totaled, I can't imagine more time, travel, and money have ever been expended in getting just three pages Xeroxed. How much money, you ask? Oh, just take an ordinary rate from Kinko's and multiply by sixty or so. But then you wouldn't have Ma'aru Tangu's insights into Hausa photocopying in the Nigerian-Nigérien borderlands.

Hi! Dad gave Lawali money to buy us some mackerel but the fish seller sold his last one just as Lawali arrived. So for dinner we just had rice, salt, and soy sauce. I wanted to go straight to bed but Dad first made me brush my teeth.

It's a poor meal, indeed. In the past it was easy to pick up a Japanese tin can of sardines or mackerel from one of the ubiquitous village street vendors. I used just to open the can and plunk the processed, tomato sauce–marinated fish into a bubbling bowl of pasta or rice. But nowadays even a small can of fish is hard to come by in Yardaje. Sam nevertheless concocts another compliment about my "cooking," giving me a millionth and one unnecessary reason for loving him.

In the evening I recount our exploits in "France"—as Niger is still referred to along both sides the borderline—to the delight of friends in Yardaje. After Sam goes to bed I roam the pitch-black village—no moonlight tonight—to the shared compound of brothers Usman Kongo and Musa Tela. Usman Kongo, one of the most intelligent and intellectually curious of Yardaje's unschooled menfolk, has an allegory for me. It explains why money—a plural word in Hausa, literally meaning "cowry shells"—is like the wind.

"Friendship is greater than money," quotes Kongo. "Trust is greater than money. For when the money is all gone, all you can rely on is other people."

It is still. We are chatting in the hut of Kongo's brother, Moses the Tailor. Musa Tela, although older—he is practically a village elder—is more naïve than his younger brother. It is he who, a decade and a half ago, would ask me such questions as, "Mallam Beel, if you drive a car, do you also fly an airplane? Are you one of the Americans who walked on the moon?" But Musa has since been to Mecca and, along with the esteemed title of alhaji, by now must have gained some greater knowledge of the non-Hausa world.

Musa is stretched on his "bed," a paper-thin mattress on the floor. On a small stool lies a Koran. From a nail hangs a shirt. And that is it: these are his possessions, this is his home. I am humbled to have entered this intimate, bedtime space of Moses the Tailor and to discuss the ways of neighboring "France," the ways of man, the way to America. Usman Kongo excuses himself for a few minutes. Musa Tela is eager to hear of our horse adventures in Niger. He agrees that I did the right thing by bringing Isma'il to Africa and reclaiming his inheritance here. Brother Usman returns. It is very late, I am drowsy, but I don't want to leave this spartan sanctum. *Zance*—conversation—is precious beyond words.

A female figure, oval object balanced on head, passes in the shadows outside the hut. Usman Kongo calls out to her. Without entering, she tenders the roundish thing to Usman; he hands it to me. "For Loïza," he declares. "This calabash is for her, carved by my wife. Greet your wife with this. Extend our greetings with this. She, too, should return and see us."

20

For Sam's sake I have been playing it safe. ("Safe?" Bringing a ten-year-old to a remote, disease-ridden, doctor-less poor patch of Africa?) To date, I have not been reckless. But there is a temptation I can no longer resist, on the eve of our return to America: a wild, solo, cut-loose gallop out in the bush. Ostensibly, I am testing Sa'a's speed. In truth, I am conquering my own fears: fear of riding, fear of aging.

After I fractured my shoulder, two years earlier, at the Equestrian Club in Mauritius, Dr. Ibrahim Rawkat, a Muslim tennis partner and surgeon, insisted how lucky I was: in his long experience treating neck and spinal injuries, no other sport is as dangerous as horseback riding. As a boy who grew up watching *Superman* religiously, I have not been able to put out of my mind the image of quadriplegic Christopher Reeve, tragic victim of his own freak horse-riding accident.

For sure, I have fallen off galloping African horses in the past. Low-hanging tree branches, path-blocking rocks and logs, rainy season rivulets, snake-shy equines: all have sent me flying though the Sahelian air. Soft sandy ground broke my falls in the past; cannot I count on that same cushioning earth now?

But I was not a father then. And are my mid-forties bones as solid as were my early-thirties ones? Is it reckless, *just one day before our return home*, to take an out-of-practice chance and careen through the bush on a young, relatively untested steed? What would happen to Sam if I were immobilized? For how long would my son be stranded in this African village?

I must banish such superstitious thoughts. I have not traveled back to Hausaland, even with my son, to regress into pampered, American parental paranoia. If I am still Mallam Beel, must I not still gallop?

While struggling between fears and responsibilities, between caution and freedom, I quietly ride up to a giant baobab tree. Under it is a camel foal. Sensing the arrival of man-horse, the baby struggles to stand; mother camel steps defiantly between newborn offspring and mounted horse. I am in awe: this is what I describe to my children as a *shehechiyanu* moment, a blessed witnessing of life. Sa'a and I respectfully continue on our way

It is time to return to Yardaje. As gently as possible, I pull the reins to spin Sa'a around. In the distance, through the thick fog of Harmattan, I can just barely make out the brown adobe huts of the village. With the gentlest of stirrup kicks, Sa'a breaks out into a mad dash.

Swishing wind, pulsating blood, wizening years—all surge forth into a torrent of terror-tinged ecstasy transporting me back ten, fifteen years to when Hausaland rebirthed me. I yell out my long-suppressed cowboy yell—YEEHAWWWW!!!—and, despite the hypnotizing beat of Sa'a's legs furiously pounding the ground, hear a distant callback: "Mallam Beeeeeeeeeeeel!"

There is no holding back Sam's horse now. We careen all the way up to the western edge of the village, arriving where the junction road to Zango joins the village elementary school and infirmary. Here on main street there is already a crowd and before long I am tagged by a throng of excited kids belting out "Mallam Beeeeel! Mallam Beeeeeeeeeeeeeeeel!"

As I trot up to the center of the village, there stands before me a *yeye*, a young, "cool" villager holding an ancient camera. He aims at me; the camera flashes; he nods assuredly. It is a great photo op, no question, and I would gladly give many naira for a print. But I have little confidence that the showoff kid had actually loaded his status symbol with live film . . .

After we came home from our ride ("Mallam Beel! Mallam Beel! Isma'il! Isma'il") the tailor arrived with my new shirt and pants costume. (In Daura I had chosen the cloth and one of Dad's friends here measured me before we left for Yekuwa. The tailor also made Dad a shirt from the same material.) Kids were annoying me by staring again but now I could scare them by aiming my slingshot—one of several I got in Yekuwa—at them. It was funny. They kept trying to get in the compound, though, and that wasn't funny.

The next morning we made the best breakfast possible because it was our last in Africa. We had chocolate with matzah, honey with matzah, tea, and raw cereal. Then we went on our last horse ride together, looking for something special—yesterday, when Dad went out riding alone on Sa'a, he came upon a 1-day old camel and her mom. We didn't find them; they had moved. But we rode around and Dad taught me how to gallop. Boy, Sa'a really does fly! He's practically faster than a bullet! . . .

Chaos. Empty suitcases, possessions strewn across the mats. What to take, what to leave behind? What do I give to whom? Non-stop visitors, bidding us adieu. Who knows when Moutari Aliyu's vehicle from Kano will arrive? Will it arrive? Kids creeping into the hut to stare. Complete loss of compound control. In the middle of it all, a stranger is brought into the hut by a village acquaintance. He too stares.

"He has come all the way from Zinder to see you," the villager says, to justify this gawking man in my hut. "He heard about you and wanted to see with his own eyes. He was so curious about you and kept asking himself, 'Is he red or is he white?'"

I look at the man squatting by the doorframe. His own frame is slight, and he is a bit ragged in dress. Maybe a Bouzou, I think in passing, a slave descendant of the Tuareg warriors of Zinder. His eyes are wide and a smile freezes on his lips. Has this poor wretch really traveled over a hundred miles just to see me, a rumored Hausa-speaker of another color? Am I that much of a freak? This does not annoy me so much as the cultural-cum-financial presumption: now that he has paid me the honor of journeying so far just to see me, I am expected to foot his travel fare. Poor man: he has come at the wrong moment. With all the packing and leave-taking and son-protection, I am in no mood to perform my circus act. Let him get back to Zinder under his own steam.

There is a man wearing headphones but who isn't carrying a CD player or a tape recorder or anything. Just wants to look cool, I guess.

Sam notices the *yeye* and asks me to explain why anyone would show off with earplugs connected to nothing at all.

Leave-taking is a fine art in Hausaland. You do not just pack up and go.

As I have just done with Faralu in Yekuwa, I must give money to Mamane, my Yardaje groom, without actually "paying" him. Fourteen years ago I performed this ritual on a weekly basis and had gotten the Friday script down pat. Now, I struggle to recall the words that permit me to discreetly "thank" my village horse helper monetarily without reducing the transaction to the vulgar level of obligatory payment for services rendered.

The hut is full—it will remain crowded until our actual departure—so I call Mamane to join me behind the mud wall separating the open-air bathing and toilet area from the rest of the compound.

"You have helped us out with Sa'a these last few days. I thank you. Tomorrow, in the morning, you will return the horse of the *hakimi* back to Yekuwa." Faralu has already arrived by Land Rover; immediately after our departure, he will ride Sa'a back to Niger, back to Yekuwa: back home.

"There is now motor transport between Yardaje and Yekuwa, isn't there?"

"Yes, there is," Mamane replies, knowing the drill.

"Here, take these naira for your transport home after Yekuwa."

"*To, madalla.*" Literally, these words meaning nothing. But they are verbal lubricators, expressing agreement, thanks, pleasure, attention.

"I also want you to take my leave of your wife for me. Greet her by giving her this." I hand him more naira.

"She will hear your greeting," Mamane replies.

"And for the children, so that she can take even better care of them—take this."

"*To, madalla.*"

"Thank you, Mamane, thank you for all your help, for me and for Sama'ila." More money transfer.

It is Mamane's turn to deliver a little speech.

"Really, Mallam Beel, all these years we continue to think about you. 'Is Mallam Beel in health? When is he returning? What about Loïza?'"

Sometimes, I know, they simply wonder about me—as one of them matter-of-factly asked about "Eliyu," the Bearded One of Brooklyn, who visited me in Hausaland in 1983—"Is he still alive?"

"You must greet her for us," Mamane continues, referring to my own wife. "And you must greet Arielle. Tell them: 'We're still here in Yardaje. We're still here, in health. Allah is with us.'

"May Allah watch over you, too, " Mamane continues, "in your distant journey, all the way back to your home in America."

The decorum of village leave-taking is unfortunately offset by the poignant inescapability of "garbage" disposal.

Even in the course of ten short days, Sam and I have stacked up an enviable collection of what, in America, we unthinkingly dismiss as sheer waste: empty water bottles, empty tin cans, empty boxes and used plastic bags and packages of all sorts. In the village, though, where the only real instruments for storage are enormous clay jugs and wide-mouthed gourds, there is a high premium on small, durable, light-weight, sealable containers. In the absence of manufactured consumer objects, even the detritus from mass-produced society is highly valued.

Seared into my head are my last moments in Yekuwa fourteen years before. When I had distributed all the toys I had brought from America—miniature cars, action figures, and plastic animals—kids scavenged furiously for the crinkly plastic coverings and cardboard packages. As the children gawked and fingered the stiff paper with the strange designs and the strong but transparent material, I realized that the wrappings were no less prized than the toys themselves.

There have already been minor skirmishes among some of the kids for our used cans of tomato paste. Sam, as part of his continuing battle against juvenile privacy transgressors, has already taken to protecting the coveted tin cans, which boys convert into toys and girls fill with peanuts and then hawk from trays balanced on their heads. It is when the adults strive to maintain their dignity while laying claim to our garbage that I am humbled and embarrassed.

Middle-aged men—including sons of the chief himself—come to me in private and sheepishly intimate, "A water bottle would be quite useful for the days I have to walk to my faraway fields" or "I could more easily perform prayer ablutions if I had one of those empty containers of yours." The stress of village leave-taking is greatly compounded by the need to distribute thoughtfully that which in our "normal" life back home we thoughtlessly throw away. To display disregard for the objects that adult friends themselves value is itself disrespectful. Unless Sam and I reflect comparable appreciation for the basic possessions that our village friends covet, then we are guilty of the arrogance of the rich and the insensitivity of the profligate. But how hard it is to remain mindful of our refuse in these moments of indeterminate separation!

We said goodbye to the Sarkin Fulani—the Chief—and I played him a farewell song on my violin. I said goodbye one last time to Sa'a (sob). I knew I probably wouldn't come back in a long while so I carefully watched everything around me to remember what Africa looked like.

It's not the horse I most want Sam to remember. It's Moutari Aliyu, our patron of Tropical Motors, Kano; Alhaji Lawal, the royal Health Inspector of Daura, who renamed him Sama'ila; Mamane, my Peace Corps "boy," who gave me the precious gift of Hausa. He should forever recall our lifelong friend Lawali, university grad and schoolteacher, who painfully straddles two cultures as a humble resident of Yardaje; faithful Faralu, who chose to care for my horse rather than enrich himself with naira; our Yekuwa host Alhaji Mallam Harouna, whose unexpected letters triggered our journey in the first place.

In both villages there are people whose voice boxes (or vocal cords) can't articulate—they're practically mute. They are for that reason very expressive in their movements. Dad can converse with them, though.

May my son forever retain the images of the palaces and retainers and their Highnesses, the Kings of Daura and Magaria; the chiefs of our two humble, borderline village homes; Jagga the Praise Singer and Jamilu, Tea King–turned–Motor Car King. May he never forget Mallam Souleymane, our crippled, hand-walking, Muslim priest friend in Magaria.

In both villages there are also blind men who get around by walking around with sticks held on one end by their sons. The son turns the stick to direct the father.

May he never forget that we wandered and rode alone, Hebrew songs and prayers on our lips, through the wilderness of Hausaland; that even during Harmattan, which fatally felled our friend Jeff Metzel, we crossed borders of continent, country, and convention; and that throughout it all, despite all risks, despite all appearances, his safety was uppermost in my mind.

It's not the horse I most want Sam to remember. It's the blind men with staffs who cheerfully greeted us, the deaf-mute women who patted us in welcome, the ragged beggars whose smiles calmed and reassured us.

I felt proud leaving Yardaje this last time, as if I accomplished what I had set out to do. I was happy that I had come and sad that I had to leave. It felt like the end of a long journey in which I had learned, and done, something impor-tant. A burden of responsibility was lifted off my back. Going to Africa taught me a new view of life.

This is the major lesson that I most hope my son will retain, long after he resumes his life as a "typical American kid": the intensity of life, and the dignity of the outwardly wretched, that together we witnessed, deep in the African bush. This was our ultimate *sa'a*; this, our true Luck.

I knew I'd have to grow up for ten days, and I honestly did my best. I think now that I did a pretty good job for a beginner!